Circle of Love

by

Romaine Stauffer

Christian Light Publications, Inc.
Harrisonburg, Virginia 22802

CIRCLE OF LOVE

Christian Light Publications, Inc., Harrisonburg, Virginia 22802
©1988 by Christian Light Publications, Inc.
Printed in the United States of America

Fifth Printing, 2008

Cover by Martha Yoder

ISBN 978-0-87813-528-8

Dedicated to my five sons,
Daryl, Dale, Steven, Gene, and Gerald
with my prayers that they will
serve the Lord all the days of their lives
and be spared the heartaches
of unfaithfulness.

INTRODUCTION

Conscientious objectors have been handled differently in the various wars in which our nation has been involved. During World War I, no provisions were made for exemption or alternate service for COs. They were required to do noncombatant service. If they refused, they were kept in an army camp under guard and persecuted for their beliefs. In World War II, COs were sent to Civilian Public Service (CPS) camps. They performed such services as reforestation without pay. If they were married, their wives were left alone at home to support themselves and their children.

In both World Wars, being a CO meant hardship for the men and their families. Unless a man firmly believed in nonresistance, he found it difficult to be faithful and steadfast in his beliefs. Some men compromised or capitulated rather than suffer for the belief that participation in war violates Biblical principles of nonresistance.

By the time of the Korean War (1950-53) and the United States' involvement in the Vietnam War in the '60s, our government had designed the IW program as the way to handle conscientious objectors. It provided them with a plan for two years of alternate service in lieu of the military. Unless a person opted to go into a non-paying, church organized and operated voluntary service assignment, the two years of IW service were spent within the United States with a paying job of the draftee's choice in a hospital or other institution serving the national interest. These jobs evoked no physical danger, persecution, or financial hardship. There were dangers, however, that were just as real though they were unseen and much more subtle.

Voluntary service programs were generally well-supervised, and young men who entered them normally benefitted greatly by them. The IW program, in contrast, was loosely structured and not sufficiently supervised. Young men were thrust into strange environments, often far from home, with very few ties to the communities in which they were born and raised. They were pushed into circumstances for which they were not properly prepared. Many lives were wrecked as a result.

The faults of the IW program were numerous, and more than one category of people shares the blame for the tragic results. Often the young men themselves were not firmly rooted in their faith. It did not cost them much to be COs, and they took the privilege for granted. Church leaders, sad to say, sometimes neglected their responsibilities. They were overworked at home and not able to keep pace with the large number of young men who were drafted during these years. Parents also were often unaware of the temptations and problems their sons faced until they were already deeply entangled in the devil's web.

Ordinarily, a IW man left home with no intentions of changing. But as he was faced with situations he was not prepared to handle, he often found himself gradually becoming acclimated to his environment and compromising his principles. Not all COs did, to be sure. There were many who left IW service with their faith intact. But far too many, without meaning to, somehow found themselves in places they had never intended to go. They did not deliberately run away, but as a sheep wanders away by keeping its eyes on the grass on which it is feasting and going a step at a time, so they wandered away and were lost.

The active draft and IW program are history. But the dangers of compromise and acclimation to our society are as real and as present as they were in IW service. Mennonites have historically been a rural people. More and more we are moving off the farms and into urban settings and commercial circles. As we have more and closer contact with the world, pressures to conform increase. Today our young people face the same temptations of the IWs without leaving their home communities. We need to be alert to and aware of the tricks and traps of the father of lies who would have us believe small things are harmless and we can indulge in them without suffering any ill effects. Sin is costly. Its effects are long-lasting, and it often does irreparable damage. Only in fairy tales does everything come to a perfect conclusion and everyone live happily ever after.

All of us make mistakes in life. Some mistakes can easily be corrected and others cannot. Since I do not want to put the serious mistakes of any one person on public display, this is not the story of one person's life. It is a compilation of the experiences of many different people, both in and out of IW settings. Characters are composite ones. All locations are given fictitious names.

Being a Mennonite, descended from many generations of Mennonites dating back to the early 1600s in Switzerland, naturally I have a great love for the Mennonite Church, its teachings, and its people. It would be easy to overlook the faults and weaknesses of the Mennonite people and portray them as ideal Christians. That, however, would not be honest. The weaknesses and mistakes of the characters in this story are left intact so we can identify with them and recognize the areas in which we need to be more diligent. Will we learn from the mistakes of the past and not repeat them in the future? "Let us go on to perfection."

Romaine Stauffer

The resemblance of any character in this story to any person who is now living or has lived in the past is coincidental. Some incidents are based on actual happenings, but all characters and places are fictitious. I appeal to you to read for the purpose of comprehending the message I seek to convey without attempting to separate fact from fiction.

He drew a circle that shut me out—
Heretic, rebel, a thing to flout.
But Love and I had the wit to win:
We drew a circle that took him in!

—Edwin Markham

Chapter 1

A pleasant June breeze wafted the scent of drying hay through the open windows of the Martinsville Mennonite Church. John Shenk shifted his position on the back bench, trying to avoid the sun's glare on the page of the *Church Hymnal* he held in his hand. It was not uncomfortably warm, yet it was such a lovely day he wished he did not have to waste it all sitting in church. But the all-day meeting was a big annual affair and his parents expected him to attend all the sessions. The noon fellowship meal would be a welcome break.

John slipped the hymnbook back into place in the rack as the song ended. Although he had blended his voice with the congregation in singing all four verses of the hymn, he had barely been aware of the words. Even now he could not have named the just-finished hymn if he had been required to do it. He slouched slightly on the bench in order to be more comfortable during the morning's sermon. He hastily pulled himself erect again and politely made room for David Lehman to sit down. David was late, as usual.

John nodded a greeting as David sat down. He took this as his cue to begin the morning's visit while the sermon was in progress.

"Staying for dinner?" David inquired in a low undertone.

John nodded.

"Man! I'm starved already," David groaned. "The dinner is the best part of the day. I could use a bowl of that chili about now, and I just ate breakfast. Mom calls this a bottomless pit," he grinned as he rolled his eyes and rubbed his stomach.

"Strange," John whispered, "my mom says the same about me."

"Say!" David changed the subject. "Did you hear anything from Uncle Sam yet?"

John shook his head.

"That's a wonder! You were twenty a couple days before I was. My number came up already. Got my draft notice this week."

"Really?"

"Yup. Got to report by the fourteenth of July."

John forgot all pretense of worship. He knew he could be drafted any time, and the subject was of great personal interest to him. It was sort of like death, though not as frightening. He knew it could happen any time, but so far it had always been someone else. Yet, he knew his time had to be close if fellows a little younger than he were being called. It truly was a wonder his notice had not yet arrived.

"Where are you going to go?" John asked.

"Oh, I don't know," David replied carelessly. "I'd kind of like to get away from here for awhile. I thought of going to Colorado."

"Colorado! Why there?"

"One of my cousins went there. I'd like to travel a little and see more of the world. The way my cousin says they have a good time out there, and he is sure I could get in at the hospital where he works."

"You would be pretty far from home," John pointed out.

"You catch on quick," David winked. "I'm tired of this stuffy place. I want to get away and make my own decisions for a change without having to answer for it all the time. I figure Colorado is far enough to give me some breathing room. The draft board

13

doesn't tell us where to go—just when. This is my chance to get away, and I'm going to take advantage of it."

John was not interested in going so far away when his time came. The main reason for his wanting to be closer to home sat across the aisle and two benches forward.

John glanced over at Miriam. She was not exactly gorgeous, but her character made her beautiful. She had a gentle nature and a compassionate heart. She was just the kind of girl who would make a solid, comfortable wife for some happy man. Lately, John had sort of gotten used to the idea that the man might be himself. He had dated several girls before, but none suited him quite like Miriam Horst. He could not be absolutely certain, of course, in the six months they had dated. But the more they were together, the more he liked her company. She gave every indication of enjoying his company just as much. At this point, John thought the idea of spending life with Miriam was rather pleasant.

Miriam looked over just then and saw John's eyes upon her. Her smile revealed that fetching dimple he so admired. He thought her smiles changed her pretty face to a lovely one. It did strange things to his heart. He was beginning to allow himself to

14

admit he was in love with her. It was not an unwelcome development. She was a lot like his mother.

His gaze drifted from Miriam to his mother, sitting on the fourth to front bench with his two little sisters, one on each side of her. Ida Shenk was not perfect, to be sure. She sometimes got impatient and annoyed at little things. She was so firmly settled on her beliefs and the rightness and wrongness of certain things that John sometimes thought she was just being stubborn. But he had to admit she had a heart of gold. The joy of her life was serving her family and, through them, serving the Lord. Her homemaking skills extended beyond her own family and home to serve others in need as well. John knew that Miriam, like his mother, could be a woman with her heart in a Mary-sphere even while her feet walked in a Martha-world.

Norman Shenk had chosen well when he married Ida, though John too often took his parents and Christian home for granted. Norman provided well for the large family of four boys and three girls. He was not as quick to speak as his wife, though he seldom differed in opinion with her. Yet, he was the undisputed head of his home. She looked to him to make the major decisions, and he was

15

a competent leader for the family. His talents were recognized as well by the church, who gave him responsibility on various committees and offices in the church. He was a busy man with the combination of family, church, and farm work.

Norman and Ida taught and showed their seven children how to live and work. In the process, the children hopefully were acquiring qualities that would enable them to have happy homes of their own someday. That day was fast approaching for the oldest daughter. In less than six months Becky would leave the family to establish a new home with Ken Weaver. She had learned from her mother the homemaking skills which could make her a good wife and mother.

John was the oldest in the line of four boys who came between Becky and the two little girls. Marlin was a little more than three years John's junior. Jimmy and Carl were twelve and nine years of age. The coming of Marilyn and Carolyn three years ago had been a double surprise and joy.

Though the visiting minister was a capable speaker, John had heard little of the message. To him, the sermon dragged on and was merely a formality to be endured until the allotted time for the message expired. It was not that he disliked attending church. It was an accepted part of life, and he never would have chosen to stay home on a Sunday morning. Church was a good place to meet girls and visit with friends. Probably more than anything else he enjoyed the social hour after church.

John looked over the congregation as the minister closed his message. *Maybe David is right*, he thought as the closing hymn was announced. *Maybe it would be good to go away for awhile and see how the rest of the world lives. The way I've been raised isn't the only way to live.*

But no, he knew Miriam would not want him to go so far away. She would want him to come home often during the two years he would be required to serve. And he did not want to be so far from her, either. When his time came, he would find a place closer to home.

Oh, well! I'll cross that bridge when I get there. He dismissed the subject as he stood for the benediction with the rest of the congregation. *What I want now is a good dinner.*

Chapter 2

The old, faded blue pickup rattled across the ruts of the field lane as John came in toward the farm buildings. The load of stray bales he had collected ended the first cutting of hay. With three younger brothers at home, he felt he was not needed on the farm full time. Pop had been agreeable when John asked to take a carpenter job off the farm. The farm was a nice place to grow up, but he did not want to be a farmer all his life. Working away five days a week and helping on the farm Saturdays suited him fine, even though it had ruined his chances of getting a farm defer-ment. But he did not really mind not getting a deferment. In a way, he was looking forward to being drafted and going into IW service.

John crossed the road and stopped at the mailbox at the end of the lane. He may as well take the mail along when he went in rather than having someone else make a special trip for it later. He reached through the open window and opened the mailbox. A single business size envelope lay inside. He glanced quickly at the return address and for a split-second his senses reeled. "SE-LECTIVE SERVICE—OFFICIAL BUSI-NESS," it said in bold, black capital letters. It was addressed to Mr. John B. Shenk.

It had to be his draft notice. He had received envelopes like this before. He had registered for the draft on his eighteenth birthday, in accordance with the law. At that time he had also applied for Conscientious Objector classification. After he received and returned a questionnaire, he was granted CO status, assigned a selective service number and issued a IO draft card. Eight months ago he had complied with the order to report for his army physical. A few days later his notice of acceptability had arrived. The next step, he knew, would be the draft notice. Men were drafted according to number and last name. With the Vietnam conflict raging, it was not a matter of if, but when his number came up that his time of service would begin.

John reached for his pocketknife and quickly slit the end of the envelope. He withdrew a single sheet of paper and read:

2 July, 1966

Mr. John B. Shenk SS NO 32 21 40 710

Dear Sir:

Being in class IO you are required to perform appropriate civilian work for a period of twenty-four consecutive months in lieu of induction into the armed forces.

You have been reached in the order of selection and are liable to perform your civilian work obligation.

You are required to take the necessary action to obtain such employment by contacting approved employers. The names of employers can be obtained at any board office.

This matter should be given your immediate attention. Notify us when you have obtained employment and the date you will begin working. Also ask your employer to notify us.

If you have not obtained a job by 23 July, please contact this office. The office is open 8 a.m. to 4:45 p.m. Monday, Tuesday, Wednesday, and Friday.

For the Local Board,
(Mrs.) Beatrice Boyer
CLERK

John drew a deep breath and scanned the letter again before replacing it in the envelope and laying it on the seat beside him. A tense smile crossed his features momentarily. So this was it! In less than three weeks he would be in IW service. It was rather exciting. It never entered his mind to thank the Lord for the provisions the government made for alternate service. He just took the privilege for granted. He was glad he did not have to enter the armed forces and go to Vietnam. But he had never given much thought to his personal convictions against being part of the war machine. The church preached nonresistance, and he accepted that teaching without question. Yet, when he had received the questionnaire concerning his position as a CO, he had been unable to answer the questions about his beliefs. The Bishop had dictated all the answers. Membership in a Mennonite church was accepted by the government as proof of a nonresistant belief and such applicants were very rarely refused. Obtaining CO status was simple and easy.

"Anything interesting in the mail?" Mom asked as John washed his face and hands at the kitchen washbowl. "I saw you stopped at the mailbox."

"My draft notice." John's muffled reply

came from inside the towel.

Mom stopped her hurrying to get the meal on the table and turned quickly to face John. "Your what?"

"My draft notice," John repeated more clearly now as he flopped the towel carelessly over the rod.

The organized confusion that precedes the process of getting a family of nine to the table halted as the meaning of John's words broke through. With the exception of the two little girls, who did not understand the implications of the announcement, everyone began asking questions at once.

"How soon?" Pop asked the most important question.

"Where will you go?" Marlin asked.

"What's a draft notice?" youngest brother, Carl, wanted to know.

"Oh, John!" Becky lamented. "You might miss my wedding. And you are supposed to be in the bridal party."

John took the envelope out of his shirt pocket and handed it to his father. "I have to go by July 23," he said even as Pop read the letter for himself.

"Less than three weeks," Mom mused, looking at the calendar. How short and precious those three weeks would be! She had hoped a solution could be found to the

Vietnam conflict before John was drafted. But the situation seemed to be getting worse instead of better. She was thankful he did not have to go to Vietnam. But it tugged at her mother heart even to have him leave for IW service. He seemed so young to leave home. And with Becky being married soon, the home would seem empty quite suddenly. Never again would she have all her children under her roof and at her table every day. The years had flown so quickly, and she was reluctant to let any of them leave the protecting cover of her wings.

"Well, let's eat before the food is cold," Pop said as he folded the letter and replaced it in the envelope. "We can discuss this after we pray."

Pop took his place at the head of the table and Mom at the foot as she set down the last steaming dish. The four boys and three girls filled their usual places along the sides and bowed their heads for silent prayer. They knew the prayer was ended when Pop cleared his throat and reached for the bread.

"Did you have any particular place in mind?" Pop asked as he speared some butter and began spreading his bread.

"Not really," John answered. "David Lehman is leaving next week for Colorado. I didn't think I wanted to go so far away, but I

23

don't know where I *can* go."

"Don't go so far that you can't come home for my wedding," Becky urged. "I don't know who else we could have if you couldn't be here. And Miriam is already making her bridesmaid's dress."

"I don't think he's so worried about your wedding as he is about seeing Miriam," Marlin chuckled with a teasing poke in John's ribs. "She'll vote for a place closer than Colorado. You can be sure of that!"

"Of course I'll talk to her about it," John stated matter-of-factly. "But first I must find out what the possibilities are."

"Of course I'll talk to her about it," Marlin mimicked. "It's no fun teasing you any more. You just own up to everything. I'm afraid you're going fast. Pity Miriam's poor family! Before long they'll have to listen to 'wedding, wedding, wedding' all the time too."

"You're just jealous," John teased back.

"Who? Me? Not on your life!" Marlin protested.

"Who believes that?" John laughed. "But seriously now, Pop. How can I find out where I can go for IW?"

"I believe I'd go to the Mission Board headquarters and ask there," Pop answered. "They have a list of places available."

"That sounds like a good idea," John

agreed. "When are they open?"

"Call and find out," Pop said simply.

John made an appointment for the next Thursday evening with Luke Stoner who headed the Peace Committee at the Mission Board. He hoped Miriam would want to go with him and was glad when she agreed to accompany him for the interview.

"Did you have anything particular in mind?" Luke Stoner asked John as he took a seat behind his desk facing the young couple. "Were you interested in IW or VS service? We have some openings in several VS places just now. Voluntary Service can be a very rewarding experience."

"I was thinking of IW," John answered. He knew either route was accepted in lieu of military service. Voluntary service was all right, he supposed, but he liked getting a paycheck. If he went into VS, he would have to give up his car. He would never be able to make the rest of the payments on the small allowance he would be given in VS. "And I'd like to be near enough to home that I can come home weekends," he added.

Luke smiled understandingly. "In that case there are several places I could recommend. Here's one at Philadelphia, Pennsylvania and one at Allendale, West Virginia. Those are both general hospitals. There is also the National Agricultural Research Center at Beltsville, Maryland, just outside of Washington, D.C. Since you come from a farm, you might be interested in that."

"What kinds of jobs do the hospitals give IWs?" John asked.

"Usually they hire IWs as dietary or maintenance personnel, for housekeeping or supply departments or as orderlies. You don't need to decide now. Talk it over together and decide later. I'll give you the names and addresses of these places," Luke said and began writing the information on a pink sheet of memo paper.

John and Miriam discussed the possibilities as they headed toward her home.

"Beltsville is awfully close to Washington, D.C. If this war got worse and they started bombing the United States, Washington, D.C. would probably be one of the first cities hit," Miriam worried. "Philadelphia or West Virginia might be safer."

"I'm not sure I'd like living in a big city like Philadelphia. I've always been a country boy," John pointed out. "I'm most interested in Allendale. According to the map, that is a smaller town and it could be driven in just a few hours. I could probably come home on weekends—if I didn't have to work," he added as an afterthought. "That would depend, I suppose, on the job I'd have."

"That would suit me fine," Miriam smiled. Her tone implied a lot more than the words said.

John squeezed her hand a moment, agreeing in silent reply.

"Well, then it's settled. I'll go to Allendale next week and see what I can find," he said cheerfully.

Chapter 3

John's '65 Fairlane swung smoothly onto the exit ramp as he neared Allendale. He paused a moment at the stop sign to check the road signs with the directions Luke Stoner had given him. By following these directions, he found his way to an attractive mid-sized town located in the panhandle of West Virginia. As he rounded a curve in the shady, tree-lined street, a large brick complex to his right came into view. The sign on the well manicured front lawn left no doubt he had come to his destination. ALLEN-DALE GENERAL HOSPITAL, it said in plain, dark blue lettering.

His heart hammered as he parked the car and mounted the steps of the front entrance. He wondered what kind of reception he would be given. Were IWs welcome? How much explaining would he have to do? How many, if any, other IWs were employed here? Where would he live if he got a job here?

The lobby inside the front entrance was tastefully decorated with a slightly old-fashioned touch. John stood a few steps inside the door and looked around uncertainly. Where should he go? How did one go about applying for a job in a hospital?

"May I help you?" asked the receptionist at a desk to the side of the room.

"I have been drafted and need to begin IW service this month," John explained. "I have come to apply for a job."

"Your name, please?"

"John Shenk."

"Have a seat, Mr. Shenk." The receptionist waved towards a nearby chair. "I will ring the personnel director."

John dropped tensely into the seat indicated. His wait was short. He jumped to his feet and turned as a voice behind him said, "Mr. Shenk?"

"Yes," he answered, shaking the proffered hand of the voice's owner.

"I'm Mrs. Greene, the personnel director. Come this way, please."

He followed Mrs. Greene to her office and took the seat she indicated across the desk from her.

"Is there any specific job you are interested in?" she asked.

"Not really," he answered. "What do you have available?"

"We have an opening right now for an orderly. Next week we will have vacancies in the maintenance and dietary departments. As an orderly, you would work directly with the patients. You would have a period of training before beginning that work. The maintenance department is responsible for keeping up the grounds and buildings. It would involve cutting grass in summer, shoveling snow in winter, painting, and general upkeep. In the dietary department you would help with food preparation both for the patients and the hospital cafeteria. You would also help with kitchen cleanup after meals."

Mrs. Greene waited in silence while John considered the possibilities. Patient care did not appeal to him too strongly. And neither did the kitchen. But maintenance sounded interesting. There was a variety of work and some of it outdoors. He would not be cooped up inside the hospital all the time.

"I believe I'd like the maintenance work," he said, looking up.

"In that department you would work Monday through Friday, 8 a.m. to 5 p.m. You would have every weekend off except occasionally in an emergency such as a snowstorm when you would have to clear the parking lot. We pay $1.50 per hour for the regular forty-hour week and time-and-a-half for overtime. The hospital pays your Blue Cross coverage in full. You would be covered by workman's compensation. You would also have eight paid holidays in a year, twelve days of sick leave per year with pay after six months of service, and two weeks of paid vacation after one year. How does that sound?"

"Great!" John grinned. *A dollar-fifty an hour, paid holidays and vacations, overtime, and every weekend off!* It was more than he could have dreamed. "I'll take it."

"Good," Mrs. Greene smiled. "We have learned IWs are generally dependable and good workers. And we know they will stay with us for two years. I'm sure we will be glad to have you and hope you will enjoy being with us. I'll need some information now," she said as she picked up a form and slipped it into her typewriter.

John provided the necessary information and signed the routine forms.

"You will be needing a place to live, I suppose? Or do you already have something in mind?" Mrs. Greene asked.

"No," he said, relaxing slightly now that his future had taken more definite shape. "Do you have any suggestions?"

"We have converted the old nurses' residence on the hospital grounds here into a residence for single men. There are several vacancies in it, and you could have one of them if you care to. All your meals could be gotten in the hospital cafeteria for 50 cents per meal. We charge $15 per week for the room. These charges would all be deducted from your paycheck. But if you would rather have your own apartment, there are some for rent in town."

John considered the options momentarily. Scrambled eggs were the only thing he knew how to make. He was sure he did not want to live on eggs for two years. A cooked meal for 50 cents was a bargain. And he would not have to wash dishes, either.

"I'll have one of the other fellows come and show you the residence if you'd like to see it before you decide," Mrs. Greene offered, taking his silence for indecision.

"All right," he said.

Mrs. Greene had Sam Troyer paged. When he reported to her office, she introduced the two young men. "John, this is Sam Troyer. He came to us from Indiana and has been with our maintenance department for over a year. Sam, this is John Shenk. He will be joining the maintenance department next week. He would like to see the men's residence. Would you take him over and show him the rooms so he can decide about his living arrangements?"

"Sure thing," Sam said with a genial grin as he and John shook hands.

"Report back to me before you leave, and let me know what you decide," Mrs. Greene instructed as the two young men left her office.

By the time they reached the men's residence, John and Sam were fast becoming friends. Sam was a companionable person and made new friends easily. John was a little surprised when Sam pulled a pack of cigarettes out of his shirt pocket and lit up. But he decided it was none of his business, and he said nothing.

Sam showed John the furnished rooms in the building and mentioned several things he would need to bring if he occupied one of them. The rooms were as varied as their owners. Some were neat and tidy. Others were cluttered and unkempt. John noticed several rooms had television sets. He had been taught that the evil influence of television greatly outweighed the worthy causes it

sometimes promoted. For the spiritual protection, blessing, and testimony of the
church, television was prohibited by his
conference. But there were more liberal
Mennonite conferences which permitted
television. So he supposed the ones who had
them in their rooms must be members of the
more liberal conferences. Sam had one in his
room, but John passed it off. He knew little
about the Indiana Mennonites. He wondered where all the IWs were from. It would
be interesting learning to know them.

"Living here is cheaper than renting your
own apartment. In town the apartments rent
for about $85 a month," Sam said. "And this
is much handier, too."

"I can see that," John agreed. "It's just a
short walk to work."

"That's not the only advantage," Sam
winked.

"Yeah, no cooking or dishwashing," John
said.

"Well—that too," Sam admitted. "But
that isn't what I meant. You're pretty green
yet, but I'll bet you catch on quick."

John chuckled uncertainly. He had no
idea what Sam was talking about. "Are all the
guys living here IWs?" he asked, changing
the subject.

"All IWs," Sam assured him. "There are

34

ten IWs altogether, but some of them are married. They rent apartments in town."

"It looks all right to me," John decided.

John and Sam quickly made the return trip across the grounds back to the hospital. The hot July sun beating down made them eager to get back into the air-conditioned comfort of the hospital.

Sam uttered a low wolf whistle at a petite, dark-haired nurse going the opposite direction as the two young men approached the outer hospital doors.

"Hi, Sam." The cute girl twinkled her eyes at him. "Got a new friend? Why don't you introduce me?"

"What? And spoil it for myself?"

"You aren't the only fish in the ocean, you conceited old thing," the girl shot back prettily. "Who's the handsome prince?"

Sam shrugged good naturedly and made the introductions.

"Where have you been all my life?" the girl giggled.

John's face grew red with embarrassment.

"Cool it, Gwen," Sam came to the rescue. "The guy just got here. He's starting on maintenance with me next week. He'll be around for two years. You don't need to rush it."

"I'm just being friendly," Gwen returned

with a pert, injured air. "See you guys later. I have to run now."

John arranged to rent one of the rooms in the IW residence and was soon heading back home. The whole thing had gone a lot better than he anticipated. He had not been questioned about his CO beliefs. No hint of ridicule had been offered by anyone. The job sounded good with the pay and benefits far better than he had ever imagined. He had expected to receive a cut in pay when he entered IW. Instead of that, he was actually getting a small raise.

He realized now he had forgotten to ask about the church which the IWs attended. His parents would probably ask about it. But it did not really matter. He would be home every weekend anyway.

Somehow it did not seem quite real. Next week this time he would be living in Allendale and working at the hospital. His life had always flowed smoothly along and things sort of fell in place like a precut pattern. Now everything would be new and different. The change would be stimulating, and he was getting excited about it now. To be honest, he decided, he could hardly wait.

Chapter 4

Miriam pulled her feet under her and curled up on the corner of the sofa. She toyed with the fringe of the cushion she held on her lap. The grandfather clock cleared its throat and then struck eleven, reminding her the evening was fast coming to an end. She wished somehow time would stand still for a little while. But the old clock resumed its patient, steady ticking as the eleventh stroke ended.

The fact that this was their last date before John left to begin IW had been uppermost in both their minds all evening, though not much had been said about it. Miriam could not have explained her feelings if she had tried. Somehow a strange foreboding sat heavily in her stomach. She felt as though a beautiful part of her life was fading away.

She wanted to make the evening last as long as possible.

"I guess I'll have to go soon," John said. "I'll have to get up pretty early so I can get to Allendale in time. I can't be late for work the first day."

Now that he had opened the subject, Miriam could no longer suppress the thoughts which had been hiding behind the pretense of lightheartedness she had maintained all evening.

"Two years seems like an awfully long time to me," she said, keeping her eyes on the cushion lest they reveal more than she was sure she wanted them to show.

"It seems long to me, too," he agreed. "But time usually goes faster than it seems it will when you are looking into the future. At least I won't be very far away. You'll hardly miss me."

"That isn't true," she protested.

"But I'll be home every weekend," he said. "We will be dating every Saturday and Sunday just like always."

"Will it be 'just like always' though?" Her voice trembled slightly.

"Of course. Why shouldn't it be?" He was a little puzzled.

"Oh, I don't know. It's just . . . well . . . I guess I'm afraid you might change and not be the same as you are now."

"I'm just starting a new job, that's all. The only difference is it's further away, and we'll never get to see each other during the week. Maybe you could come some weekend and see the place."

"That would be nice." Her eyes lit up as she got to her feet. "Since we are alone tonight, why don't you come along out in the kitchen? We could have some lemon meringue pie before you go."

"You know I'd never turn that down," he grinned. "This is the only place I've ever had lemon meringue pie as good as Mom's."

"I knew it's your favorite. That's why I made it for tonight," she smiled.

As John drove towards Allendale early the next morning, he had plenty of time to think. And his thoughts automatically turned to Miriam and their date the evening before. Time spent with her was never wasted. With her, he felt every inch a man. She made him want to do his best to be someone she would admire. He could not understand her anxiety about his leaving. He thought she acted like she was sending him off forever instead of only for five days. But he supposed women just naturally worried more than men. After a few weeks, she would get used to the idea.

Miriam was not the only one to voice concern about his leaving. News travelled fast, and several people at church Sunday morning had spoken to him about it. They seemed glad to hear he would be back every weekend. His parents said little, but he knew he would not soon forget Mom's gentle concern. Although he had told her it was not necessary, she had gotten up early to see him off when Pop went to the barn.

"Are you sure you have everything you'll need?" she asked as he opened the screen door to go out to the car with the last load of his things.

"If I don't, I'll make the best of it until I come home again," he had replied.

There was so much more she wanted to say. But her tremulous heart fluttered, and the words were stillborn on her lips. There was a stubborn knot in the apron strings of her mother's heart that she found difficult to open. Just yesterday, it seemed, he had come to her with all his little boy problems and now he was going away beyond the shelter of her wings. How could she let him go?

"Well . . . be careful then," she said, looking deep into his eyes.

"I will. See you Saturday," he had promised. He knew by the pathos in her eyes she meant more than just driving carefully. He could not have understood her feelings any better than she could have expressed them. He was a young man going off on an adventure. She was a mother seeing the first of the brood leave her and wondering if he was ready to go.

It was still early when John parked in the hospital parking lot. He had allowed plenty of time for the driving and had encountered no difficulty. When it was nearly eight o'clock, he reported to the receptionist and officially changed his draft status from IO to IW.

Most of the morning was spent getting orientated. John received a meal ticket entitling him to one free meal a day in the cafeteria during his working hours. For him, this was the noon meal. He was also measured for the dark blue uniforms maintenance personnel wore and issued an ID pin which he was to wear while working. It identified him both by name and department.

When all the formalities were attended to, John was introduced to Joe Martino, the maintenance supervisor. Joe set John to work with Sam, painting a room in the east wing that was being remodeled for some new diagnostic equipment. John was glad to have

Sam as a working partner rather than one of the other two men in the maintenance department. They were older, local men. John felt more comfortable with Sam.

The layout of the hospital seemed like a maze. John wondered if he would ever learn where everything was on all the floors. He was glad he could trail Sam to the cafeteria at noon. *I probably would have spent the whole noon hour hunting the place*, he thought ruefully.

Following Sam's motions, John pushed a tray along the rail and filled it. He trailed Sam to a table where the other two men from the maintenance department were sitting and set his tray down. As he slid into his seat, he automatically bowed his head. He was well into his mental prayer before he was aware that Sam had not followed suit. John ended his prayer in mid-sentence. Looking up, he saw the amusement in the other men's eyes and was embarrassed. He quickly lowered his eyes and began eating as if nothing was amiss.

John was glad when quitting time came. It was a relief to get away from the constant racket of Sam's radio. He did not know how Sam could enjoy the noise, as he obviously did. But it was a free country after all, and if Sam wanted to listen to the Beatles, it was his privilege.

It did not take John long to arrange in his room the things he had brought from home. When he finished making the bed, it did not look quite right somehow. He had a terrible time getting the pillow into the case. He did not know what he was doing wrong, but he finally decided to call it good enough and let it go. He had always taken clean sheets for granted. He never knew any kind of skill was needed to make a bed correctly from the bottom up.

The days began to take on a pattern as the week progressed. He found he could sleep later than he was used to and still easily make it to work on time. He usually ate his evening meal right after finishing the day's work. The evening hours were free to do whatever he pleased. He had brought some books from home and planned to catch up on some reading he had been wanting to do. He soon learned the unwritten code of the group was a closed door on anyone's room meant the occupant wanted privacy, and an open door was an invitation for anyone to come in and pass the time. The other fellows took advantage of John's usually open door to come in and get acquainted.

The number of fellows in the building on any given evening depended on the departments in which they were employed and the shifts they worked. Over the week, John learned to know the ones who were usually free weekday evenings as well as a few who had part-time evening jobs. One fellow was a Quaker, and another belonged to the Church of the Brethren. John was surprised when he learned Sam was Amish, although he knew he should have guessed as much by the sound of his name. It was nice to have his own room where he could retreat if he wanted privacy and yet have other fellows around when he wanted company. John was glad he had not rented his own apartment in town.

By Friday afternoon it seemed like a long time since he had been home. The meals in the cafeteria were well-balanced and nutritious, but they did not taste like his mother's cooking. He had planned to go home Saturday morning. But he realized now he could easily make the trip right after work and arrive well ahead of bedtime. The more he thought of going home, the more impatient he was for quitting time so he could leave.

All the way home he imagined how surprised his family would be to see him. He was not disappointed. The twins mobbed him as he walked in the door. He could see

44

everyone was surprised and pleased with his early return. After he had answered all the questions about Allendale and his work, John leaned back in the recliner. Only now, as the familiar routine of the family beginning to get ready for bed swirled around him, did he realize how very much he had actually missed the family circle. It was good to be home. It felt good to climb the stairs and sink into his own familiar bed in the room he and Marlin shared. He had two full days of Mom's cooking ahead of him and two evenings with Miriam before he had to think of another week in Allendale.

Chapter 5

The second week in Allendale was not nearly as strange and long as the first one had been. Slowly John was becoming familiar with each floor of the hospital and could find his way around alone. Although he did not want to make it a lifetime career, he enjoyed the work sufficiently so the two years would not be unpleasant. Life soon settled into a routine of working five days and going home for the weekends.

As he grew better acquainted with the other IWs, John spent less and less time in his room with the books he had planned to read. He still intended to read them sometime, but he just never seemed to get around to it. If he did start reading, one of the fellows popped in to ask if he wanted to go along to the K-Mart. Or they might go to

McDonald's for supper for a change from the hospital food. They often sat in the lounge playing Rook and talking. Somehow, he never got down the hall to his room until past bedtime.

Gradually, John learned how loosely Sam was living. He made no secret of his popularity among the nurses. His smoking and drinking was nothing more than a big joke to him. He seemed to think it was natural to sow some "wild oats," as he called it. He was far from home, and with no one to draw the lines, he did as he pleased.

The church, which John had taken for granted would be there, was non-existent. Some of the married couples met together in one of their apartments on Sundays for their own worship service. But there was no organized church or resident minister to oversee the IWs. Though the single fellows were all welcome to join in the married couples' worship, not all of them did. Some were not interested; others did not always have Sundays off. John went home every weekend.

In spite of his loose living, Sam was such a friendly fellow everyone liked him. He would do anything for anyone, even going out of his way to help someone. He was a good worker and was well liked by the supervisor. John soon got so used to Sam's ever-present radio he often was not aware it was on. Some of the hit tunes were sort of catchy, and John found himself humming along with them. It really was not so bad once he was used to it.

The hospital's big annual September Fair was held about six weeks after John began work. All proceeds from the affair were for the benefit of the hospital. The maintenance department had a lot of extra work getting ready for the gala event which was held on the expansive lawn. Tents and booths were set up to protect the displays and concession stands. At the conclusion of the week-long affair, a dinner dance would be held in a banquet hall across town. It was a mark of prestige to be invited to the dance. John neither expected nor desired to attend. His participation in the whole thing extended no further than the maintenance work involved.

"We had a pretty heavy rain last night," Joe said as John and Sam reported for work on Friday. "Quite a bit of water collected along the edges of the main tent. I want you two to go around the tent and empty the water before the people start coming today. We don't want any of our customers to have an unexpected shower on the last day of the fair, or they might not come back next year," he joked.

"Okay," Sam agreed quickly. "Bring that

broom, John."

John poked the broom handle under the sagging portion of the tent to support it while Sam tilted the canvas, allowing the water to run to the ground. Together they went around the tent, emptying the pockets of rain water.

"Good morning, handsome," a saucy voice sang out.

John and Sam turned to see Gwen behind them.

"At your service, ma'am," Sam said in mock graveness and bowed low.

"Oh, I didn't mean you," Gwen returned. "You're not as handsome as your helper, you conceited thing. But since John seems to be tongue-tied around women, I guess I'll have to be satisfied with you." Gwen gave John a look that clearly said, *Come on. Don't be bashful.*

"What are you doing out here anyway?" Sam ignored the slam.

"That's what I asked myself this morning when the old buzzer rang," Gwen giggled. "It's my day off and I could've slept in. But you know what a sucker I am. Good old kindhearted me had to go and promise to sell raffle tickets today. Loyal employee of Allendale General, dedicated to the nursing profession and all that, you know."

"Sam, you are going to be my first customer. One dollar, please."

"Sure, sure," Sam laughed, taking out his wallet. "And just to show how dedicated to Allendale General I am, I'll buy two tickets. And don't forget John here."

Gwen took Sam's two dollars and handed him the tickets in return. "Thank you, sir." She turned her most charming smile on John. "And how many for you?"

"Uh . . ." John stammered, "isn't that gambling?"

"Oh, come on! Don't be such a goody-goody!" Sam exploded. "This isn't gambling. It's a donation to the hospital."

"Well . . ." John considered. "If you look at it that way, maybe it isn't gambling. Oh, all right. I can spare a dollar for a good cause," he suddenly decided and reached for his hip pocket. "Oops! Forget it. I don't have a cent on me. I must have left my wallet in my room."

"Give the poor guy a ticket. It's on the house," Sam said, taking another dollar from his wallet.

John took the ticket, put it in his shirt pocket and promptly forgot about it.

When he returned to work Monday morning, Sam was waiting for him. "Hey! Nobody claimed the prize in the raffle yet. Do you still have your ticket? You might be the winner."

"I doubt it," John said. "I don't even remember what I did with the ticket. Oh, yes! I put it in my shirt pocket because I didn't have my wallet. It's probably still there."

"Let's go see," Sam urged. "The suspense is killing me."

"It can wait until lunch." John was not excited.

"But it will only take a minute to run into your room and get it."

"Oh, all right, if you're so impatient. But it's no winner anyway."

"What's the number?" Sam asked as John found the ticket.

"Z21058," John read.

Sam stared. "Run that by me again."

"Z21058," John repeated.

"That's it! You won!" Sam yelled.

"You're kidding! I never won a thing in my life."

"You did now. You just won a brand new floor model color TV. Let's go turn in this ticket and claim it."

John's mind raced. *A color TV!* What would he do with it? It was out of the question to take it home. And he could not have it in his room if he got company from home. He had to get out of this somehow.

"But I can't take it," he faltered. "I mean . . . it isn't mine. You paid for the raffle ticket. It's really yours," he finished.

"Mine . . . yours . . . what's the diff?" Sam breezed. "We live in the same pad. We'll put it in the lounge, then everybody can enjoy it. How does that grab you?"

"Uh—okay, I guess," John agreed lamely.

The furniture in the lounge was easily arranged around the new TV. Sam thought it was all a good joke and got a kick out of calling it "John's TV." John was always quick to remind Sam it was his dollar that bought it. And so the handsome appliance stood in the center of the lounge, not really claimed by anyone, but enjoyed by most of the young men. John himself was not overjoyed by its presence. It gave him an uneasy feeling. As long as it was not in his room, he could easily disclaim any ownership if Miriam or his parents visited. But what if one of the others said "John's TV," as they often did? How could he explain it?

Oh, well! I'll cross that bridge when I get there, he decided. *No use worrying about something that might never happen.*

Packing his small suitcase to go home for the weekend had become so routine John could do it quickly. He did not need much for a weekend. His suit was kept at home for Sundays. He closed the lid and snapped the clasp on the suitcase. Picking it up, he started for his car. At the front door he stepped aside to let Sam enter.

"Going home again?" Sam more stated than asked, noting the suitcase.

"Yeah."

"You go home every weekend. Why don't you stay over sometime?"

"You know why."

"Yeah, I know why. You have a girl you must go see. There are girls around here too, you know. Or haven't you noticed? Gwen is just dying to go out with you."

"I know," John admitted. "But I'm not interested. Miriam is a nice girl, and I don't want to fool around and spoil what I have."

"Suit yourself," Sam shrugged. "But I'll bet Gwen would treat you better than your girl at home." He winked.

"Take her out yourself then. I'm going home," John called back as he went down the steps.

"*Such* a good boy!" Sam teased, shaking his head in mock unbelief.

John felt foolish and was ashamed of himself for being embarrassed. There was really no reason to be ashamed of Miriam or his feelings for her. But he did not like to be laughed at or have anyone think he was a goody-goody.

One look at Miriam's face as she opened the door for him Saturday evening convinced him of the rightness of his faithfulness to her. A giddy, flirty girl like Gwen could never hold a candle to Miriam.

As he crossed the threshold and closed the door behind him, Miriam wrinkled her nose. "Phew! That smoke smell gets stronger on you all the time."

"Sorry about that. I guess I'll have to use a whole bottle of Aqua Velva next time," John joked.

"Why don't you get rid of the cigarettes instead?" Miriam said. Though her tone was a bantering one, John knew what she was implying.

"Oh, let's not start our evening that way," he pleaded. "You bring this up every weekend lately. I can't help it if my clothes pick up the smoke smell. That's just what happens when you live with smokers. I *told* you I don't smoke. Never have and don't intend to start now. You don't think I'd lie to you, do you?"

"No," Miriam said slowly, sounding only half sure. "But I can't help but wonder, the way you smell."

"So if you don't like it, you'll just have to

lump it. I can't help it." John shrugged rudely and changed the subject.

An uneasy truce prevailed the balance of the evening. As she got ready for bed after John had gone home, Miriam reflected on the evening. She blamed herself for the poor start they had. She guessed she *had* brought up the smoking subject pretty often lately. But John had never acted as irked and hurt about it as he had tonight. She tried her best to make Sunday evening pleasant for both of them. The uneasy feeling of the previous evening was gone and she wondered if perhaps she had been making mountains out of molehills. Maybe he had not been as irked as she had imagined. He seemed to have forgotten it happened.

"Do you think your parents would bring you to Allendale for a weekend sometime after Becky's wedding?" John asked as the time neared for him to leave on Sunday evening.

"Are you sure you want me to come?" she asked.

"I wouldn't have asked if I didn't. Why wouldn't I?" he asked, sensing the undercurrent in her words.

"Oh, I don't know. Are you sure you want all your pretty nurses to see your home-grown girl?" she teased. She expected him to turn her words around as he often did and say something about the privilege it would be for the nurses to see how pretty the homegrown girls were. But he took quite another meaning from her words.

"None of the nurses are *mine*," he objected. "What makes you think I'd be a two-timer?"

"Oh! I didn't mean . . ." she faltered. She could not say what she had meant. "But I'm sure the nurses aren't all blind," she plunged on without thinking. "I mean, when such a good-looking guy like you comes along, there must be oodles of them trying to chase you down."

"If that were true I'd never get any work done. I'd spend all my time dodging the flirts."

"So there *are* some after you then?" she probed. Her smoldering jealousy and fear of other girls ate away her resolve to keep the evening pleasant.

John hesitated before answering. He knew they were back on dangerous ground, but he could not truthfully say "No." Every split second he hesitated fed Miriam's suspicions.

"Not *some*," he said at last. "Just one. But she is a giddy flirt, and I'm not inter-ested. I'm always trying to dodge her. As long as I have you to come home to, nobody else interests me."

"Do some of the other fellows date nurses?" Miriam asked.

"Yes," he had to admit. "Some of them. But they do more things I don't do."

"Like what?"

"Like smoking. You know that already."

"Is that all?"

"No," he said slowly. "I don't want to squeal on anybody. But if you come to visit, you'll see some of this stuff anyway. Some of the guys live pretty loosely. They take out girls all the time. Sometimes they come home drunk. They have TVs in their rooms and there is one in the lounge, too," he confessed, stopping short of explaining how it came to be there.

Until now Miriam's fears had simply been imagination. But to hear John so plainly state the facts chilled her. She lost all sense of caution and without considering the consequences blurted bitterly, "So you spend your evenings watching TV and drinking."

"I don't drink," he said, hurt showing plainly. "I do watch TV sometimes. I mean, there we all are, sitting in the lounge and it's on. It's pretty hard not to watch it. You would too if you were me."

"Depends what you watch," she said absently. "What all else do you do that you never told me?"

"Don't you trust me at all, Miriam?" he asked. "If you don't trust me it doesn't matter what I say. You won't believe me anyway. I'm not living a double life if that's what you think. It's up to you if you want to believe me or not."

Miriam was silent.

"Do you trust me, Miriam?" he prodded.

"Yes," she said hesitantly as though trying to convince herself she really did. "I guess I'm afraid of what could happen to you when you live with people like that. We get like the people we're around, you know."

"Then I'll stick close to you," he said consolingly.

She smiled shakily. "I'm sorry I ruined the evening again."

"That's all right, if you feel better," he forgave her.

As he returned to Allendale early the next morning, John pondered the difference of the two worlds in which he lived. At home and in church on weekends, things were the same as they always had been. During the week at Allendale, he was in a different world. The men he worked with thought and talked differently than the ones at home. He could slip easily from one world to the other and back again. He could be a part of the

group at Allendale without becoming involved in anything serious, he was sure. He
felt comfortable in both worlds.

Chapter 6

"I finished my dress this week for Becky's wedding," Miriam said on the way home from the Saturday evening young people's meeting. "Becky picked such nice fall colors for her bridal party. Can you believe it's only a week until the wedding?"

"It's not coming fast enough for Becky," John grinned. "She's counting the days."

"You won't forget to get a haircut before next Saturday, will you?" Miriam reminded him.

"No, I won't forget," he said irritably.

She glanced at him quickly. "Well . . . I just noticed tonight your hair is getting pretty long. It comes down over your collar," she tried to explain.

"How could I forget?" he nearly snapped. "Ever since I got home last night someone or other has been bugging me about it."

"I'm sorry," she apologized meekly. "No offense intended. I wouldn't have mentioned it if I had known you were already reminded."

"Aw, forget it," he apologized lamely in return. "I'll get a haircut and come to the wedding looking like a good little Mennonite."

"What do you mean by that? What's wrong with looking like a Mennonite?" she bristled.

"Nothing at all," he replied mockingly. "Shall I wear a big black hat, too?"

Miriam did not answer. Her heart sank. They were at it again. Why did they spoil every date lately with a spat? How did these things ever begin? The least little thing seemed to set them at each other, and before they knew it, they had either implied or said things they did not really mean. What had come between them?

John matched Miriam's silence as he drove the last mile to her home. He wondered how their formerly happy relationship could have soured so badly. Before he had gone into IW he had been fairly certain Miriam was the girl for him. He could not put his finger exactly on any one thing that started it, but gradually a wall seemed to have gone up between them. She seemed to be suspicious of everything he did or said. Her extreme jealousy and possessiveness grated on his easy-going nature. The weekends were becoming more miserable, and he was beginning to wonder if it was worth the trouble of coming home every weekend if they got into an argument every time. He was getting tired of handling her with kid gloves. He wondered if she was trying to coerce him into an engagement. If that was her idea, he thought, she was going at it all wrong. The more jealous and possessive she became, the less he was attracted to her. He did not want to live with a woman who nagged and needled him at every turn. If it were not for Becky's wedding, he would be tempted to stay in Allendale next weekend. Maybe if he did not see her for awhile, he would know better how he felt about their relationship.

The day of Becky and Ken's wedding dawned clear and crisp. The bright October sun soon evaporated the early morning chill. It was a perfect day for a wedding. Becky had gone to great pains to make sure every detail of the wedding was perfect. From the warm fall tones of the dresses of the girls in the bridal party to the choosing of the wedding text and music, nothing had been overlooked. The hour-and-a-half wedding service proceeded without missing a beat. Becky's face was radiant, but her eyes shimmered with tears as she took the arm of her beaming husband at the close of the ceremony. Together, they took the first steps of their new lives as they made the short trip to the back of the church. The aura of their love and the holiness of God that permeated the wedding overflowed to those present as they witnessed the joy of the holy union.

John looked into Miriam's eyes as they met at the center of the aisle. The hints of gold in her brown eyes were enhanced by the simple gold dress she wore. Her brown hair was neatly and attractively arranged under her white covering. Her face was flushed with the excitement of the wedding. Her heart was in her eyes as she smiled up at John and took her place beside him to follow Ken and Becky back the aisle.

John returned the smile and the message with his own eyes. He wanted for himself the happiness Becky and Ken so surely had. He knew now no one could fill that need like Miriam. Whatever had been the matter with them lately was in the past. From here on they would begin anew. Someday it would be Miriam in white on his arm leading the procession back the aisle.

The dinner served for the reception was

tastefully prepared and served, but John
remembered little of what he ate. Eating in
front of several hundred people was a rather
uncomfortable experience. He was glad
when the mints were passed and the Amen
of the last prayer had been spoken. But then
the bridal party was kept busy posing for
pictures.

"My face is stiff from smiling so much,"
Miriam said with relief when the last flash-
cube popped.

"You needed the practice," Ken teased.
"You'll be the bride before long. Isn't that
right, John?"

"Wouldn't you like to know?" John
laughed noncomittally.

The wedding kept John and Miriam under
its spell all weekend. For the first time in
many weeks they enjoyed a whole weekend
without one disagreement. John went back
to Allendale happier than he had been for a
long time. He was actually looking forward
to seeing Miriam the next weekend instead
of dreading it as he had begun to do lately.

The week plodded along routinely. On
Tuesday evening the usual group sat in the
lounge idly preparing to play poker. There
was nothing else to do. John deftly shuffled
and dealt out the deck of cards. He laughed
mentally at himself to think how awkward he

had felt the first time he had held a hand of Rook cards and had to be taught how to play the game. He had learned quickly and had moved on to master other card games. His conscience jabbed him when they added coins to the game, but its voice was drowned out by the excitement of the chance of winning.

The phone rang, and John picked it up since he was sitting nearest to it. "Hello."

"Is Samuel there?" the voice on the other end of the wire asked.

"Samu—oh! Sam Troyer?"

"Yes. Is he there?"

"Just a minute . . . It's for you," John said, handing the phone to Sam.

Sam took the phone gingerly. Some sixth sense seemed to warn him of trouble ahead. His answers to the questions asked by the caller were given in the Pennsylvania Dutch dialect and were brief. John had never given it a thought that Sam would be able to speak Dutch. It was amusing to hear, although John could not understand what Sam said.

"John, would you mind taking me down to the bus station?" Sam asked as he replaced the phone on its hook.

"Why? What's wrong with your car?" John asked in surprise.

"Nothing . . . except . . . Look, I might

as well explain," Sam said wryly. "That was my Pop. Mom and Pop went to Pennsylvania for a funeral. They decided to stop in to see me on their way home. They're down at the bus station and called to see if somebody could come pick them up. I'm Amish, remember? I don't have a car."

"Oh! Sure. I'll take you down," John agreed, getting up. "I don't have anything to do that can't wait."

"I have to get ready first," Sam called back as he started down the hall.

"What's he doing? Housecleaning?" John joked as a variety of muffled thumps and scraping noises issued from Sam's room.

"Probably something like that," one of the others grinned. "Poor guy. He didn't have much warning."

The car was not the only thing Sam had to hide, John suddenly realized. He would have to get rid of his TV, radio, camera, magazines, and records. But even this knowledge did not prepare him for the transformation that soon appeared in the doorway of Sam's room. There stood an embarrassed young Amishman, complete with lavender shirt, broadfall pants, suspenders, center-parted hair, and a broad-brimmed black hat.

The moment of shocked silence was broken when one of the fellows slapped his knee and bent over, convulsed with laughter.

"Sam! I never would have believed it!" he guffawed. "Where were you keeping all that stuff?"

"Aren't you a little early for the Halloween party?" another kidded.

"Isn't he cute?" another laughed, reaching out and snapping Sam's suspender.

"Aw, lay off," Sam growled miserably. "Let's go, John."

John could not stop the amused grin that spread over his face. But at the same time he felt sorry for Sam. All evening and the next day until Sam's parents left, John witnessed Sam's humiliation. Who could have thought the self-confident, arrogant Sam everyone knew could become this quiet, plainly dressed, Pennsylvania Dutch speaking Amishman? He was aware of the stares and whispers that followed in his wake as he complied with his parents' wishes and showed them around the hospital. He lived and died a thousand deaths in those 24 hours. His real life was kept carefully under cover as those who knew him best maintained a taciturn silence at his obvious embarrassment at being seen as he now was.

No man can serve two masters, John thought to himself as he understood Sam's plight. If Sam had appeared to his parents the way he really was, he would have been in trouble. But by trying to fool them, he had blown his cover on the other side of his life.

Whatever I am, I'll never be a hypocrite, John decided.

Chapter 7

Sam's relief at saying good-by to his parents was plainly evident when he returned them to the bus depot. It was amazing how quickly the old Sam returned, although it would be a long time before he heard the last of the teasing. Indeed, Sam assumed an even greater "so-what" attitude than he had before. To prove he was the same old Sam, he threw a party the next week. Sam had often bragged about his weekend parties, but John was not fully prepared for the intensity of the boisterous party that swirled around him in the lounge. He had never witnessed first-hand the lengths to which Sam would go. Was he always like this? John wondered. Or was he working overtime to impress them with how hip he was?

The girls were plentiful, and Sam could

have his pick. They nearly threw themselves at him. The booze flowed freely and the room was soon thick with smoke. Someone started dancing, and the volume of the noise increased as the laughter and music intertwined. Some of the girls brought their boyfriends. There were many people John did not know. He was surprised at how large the party had grown. Sam obviously had gained a reputation for his parties.

Seeing another opportunity to beguile John, Gwen had come and was making him miserable as he tried to beat off her advances. He sat in a corner, sipping the ginger ale he had taken in place of the harder drinks available. He watched the dancers swirl by in the crowded room.

"Aren't you going to dance with me?" Gwen asked enchantingly as she slipped onto the arm of his chair. "You don't make a good wall flower."

"Sorry. I don't know how to dance," John admitted frankly.

"Is that all? Well, I'd love to teach you." Gwen stood in front of him and held out her hand coaxingly.

"No, thanks."

"Why not?" Gwen pouted prettily.

"Because I have a girl at home. I told you that before."

Gwen swore impatiently. "Don't be such a goody-goody. You need to have a little fun sometimes. Nobody will tell on you. Come on."

John shook his head. *If she does not soon stop, I will have to dance with her just to get rid of her,* he thought. He picked up his can of ginger ale and took a sip. A puzzled frown creased his face. He looked at the can and took another sip. Gwen giggled. John looked up to see several people watching him. Suddenly, he knew what had happened. While she kept him occupied, someone else had poured some of their drink into his can.

Just then Gwen seated herself seductively on John's lap. "I'm going to show you how to have fun," she twinkled up at him. "I know you'd enjoy yourself if you'd just let yourself go a little." Before he could reply she wrapped her arms around his neck and kissed him.

"Got 'cha," Sam chortled as a flash bulb popped.

John jumped to his feet, dumping Gwen and his soda can unceremoniously on the floor. His face turned red with anger and embarrassment. "You stooge!" he spat out and started down the hall towards his room. The crowd was getting tipsy. He'd had enough!

"Hey! Where are you going?" Gwen cried in dismay. "You can't leave now. We're just getting started."

John did not answer. He continued down the hall and escaped to the privacy of his room. He knew Gwen would soon find someone else on which to practice her charms. She took anyone she could get, although she seemed to regard the IWs, and him in particular, as prey to be stalked. To her, the IWs were an intriguing oddity and something to be bagged like big game.

The noise of the party made sleeping impossible. John lay staring at the darkened ceiling for a long time until the noise of the party finally quieted in the wee hours of the morning.

Sam did not appear the next morning at the usual time. John did not wait, but went to work alone.

"Sam called in sick this morning," Joe told John. "Sounded to me like a little too much party."

John's anger burned all day, but by quitting time his fury had subsided enough that he did not lose control when he demanded of Sam an explanation for the incident the night before.

"I'm sorry. Really, I am," Sam apologized

humbly. "I didn't think you'd take it seriously. I guess it *was* a stupid thing to do."

"When you get that film developed, I want that picture. Nobody is going to see that one," John vowed.

"Sure, sure," Sam agreed. "I don't want it. You can have it."

Sam was as good as his word. The developed pictures arrived on a Friday afternoon. John was just getting into his car to leave for the weekend when Sam came up to the car. He shuffled the pack of pictures he held and handed one through the window to John.

"Here you are. Sorry about that," Sam apologized again.

"Aw, forget it," John forgave him. "I know you wouldn't have done it if you hadn't been stoned. Thanks for giving it to me. I'll get rid of it as soon as I can, and that will be the end of it."

John tore the picture in two and threw the pieces into the glove compartment before he backed out of his parking space and headed for home. The trip was so routine he thought he could almost have done it in his sleep.

As he drove in the lane at home, his headlights picked up the familiar sight of Ken's car parked near the house. *Ken and Becky are home from their honeymoon!* John jumped out of the car and ran up the front steps. The next minute he was thumping Ken on the back and saying, "Good to see you, old buddy! How's married life?"

Ken and Becky were glad to be home again though they had enjoyed their trip to Florida immensely. It was late when the happy newlyweds set off for their own home not far away.

John picked up Miriam right after breakfast the next morning. They were to be waiter and waitress at the wedding of one of her cousins which was a two-hour drive away. Miriam seemed to be making extra efforts since Ken and Becky's wedding to make their times together pleasant ones. If the forced cheerfulness was a bit strained and unnatural, it was much better than the cold war they had waged previously.

The crew of waiters and waitresses left the wedding as soon as possible in order to attend to their duties in the last-minute preparations for the reception. The waitresses placed dishes of nuts, mints, and relishes on the tables while the waiters set chairs around the tables.

"Are we supposed to light the candles?" one of the waitresses asked.

"Yes, but not until just before the reception begins," the head waitress said. "Does anyone have matches? I haven't seen any around."

"I think John might have some in the car," Miriam said. "I'll go and see."

She dashed out to the car and opened the ash tray where he often had a pack of matches along with some loose change and a few odds and ends. No matches. Maybe there were some in the glove compartment. Hastily, she opened it and looked inside. A torn photograph lay on top of the tidy pile of contents. She held the pieces together and stared at it. A stupefying horror seized and then overwhelmed her. The picture was not very good quality, but the one person was unmistakably John. He was sitting on an armchair with a can in his hand. A girl on his lap was kissing him. Miriam's hands shook and turned clammy. She threw the picture back in the glove compartment as if she had been burned and slammed the lid. Woodenly, she returned to the dining hall.

"Did you find some?" the other waitress asked.

"Find some?" Miriam asked stupidly. She shook her head as if to clear it. "Oh! No. No, I didn't find any," she answered absently.

The girl looked at her quickly. "Are you all right? You look pale."

With an effort, Miriam pulled herself together. She had to act natural. "I—uh—something sort of came over me for a minute," she stammered. "I'll be all right."

"Shall I get John?"

"No! No, don't get John," Miriam nearly panicked.

"All right, if you say so. But you'd better sit down for awhile. You look like you saw a ghost."

"Maybe I did." Miriam tried to laugh and failed.

Chapter 8

The rest of the day was a blur. Miriam never knew how she managed to get through it. But John was not fooled. He knew something had happened to turn the gaily chattering girl of the morning into the silent and aloof one he escorted home in the late afternoon. His inquiries brought only short, inconclusive answers.

"I have a splitting headache," Miriam said truthfully as John helped her take off her coat when they got home. "If you don't mind going home, I think I'll go to bed."

"Shall I come back later," he asked cautiously.

"I guess not. I'm afraid I wouldn't be very good company anyway," she answered, avoiding his eyes.

"Are you sure a headache is all that's the

matter?" he probed.

"Have *I* ever lied to *you*?" she burst out.

"Not that I know of."

"And I'm not lying now. I have a frightful headache."

"I'm sure there is something else. But if you won't talk, I can't make you."

"Oh! Just go away and let me alone," she wailed.

"If it's that bad . . ." He turned and opened the door. "I'll say good night, then."

"Good-by," she said tonelessly.

Without understanding why, John felt like a whipped puppy slinking away with its tail between its legs as he walked to the car. Miriam's behavior had become a puzzle to him. He never knew quite what to expect anymore. That morning she had been purring like a contented kitten, and by afternoon she was practically snarling like a tiger. He sighed and wondered if he would ever understand her. Just when they seemed to have made a new beginning, now they were in worse trouble than ever before.

John spent a troubled evening at home. He explained his presence to his family by saying Miriam was not feeling well and wanted to go to bed. He looked for her in vain at church the next morning.

"Where's Miriam?" he asked her little

brother after church was dismissed.

"At home," the boy said. "She's sick."

"Would you give her a message for me?"

"Sure."

"Tell her to call me if she feels better and wants me to come over this evening."

"I'll tell her."

The telephone hung silently on its hook all afternoon. John was tempted to call Miriam himself, but at last decided against it. She could call if she wanted him to come. After the cold shoulder she had given him yesterday, he was not going to go where he was not welcome. When it was so late in the evening that he knew she would not call, he decided to leave for Allendale. *If you want to be that way, be that way,* he thought in annoyance.

The mystery unraveled on Wednesday with the arrival of a letter from Miriam. It was not unusual for her to write to him during the week, but he was especially impatient to see what she had to say this time. Would she explain, apologize, or what? He tore open and quickly scanned the short note. There was no endearing salutation. It said simply:

John,

On Saturday I went to look for some matches in your car. In the glove compartment I found proof of what I have suspected for a long time. I am very disappointed to discover you have been doing things like this behind my back and denying it. Any love I may once have had for you is gone. You need not come back.

Miriam

John's hand dropped weakly, and the letter fluttered to the floor. *So that's it! That awful picture!* In the excitement of seeing Ken and Becky home, he had forgotten it. Everything came into focus now. He understood what had made the drastic change in Miriam. He got the offensive picture, tore it to shreds and dropped it in the wastebasket. But it was too late to undo the dirty work the picture had done.

I at least owe her an explanation, he thought. *Maybe if I write and explain, she will understand.*

His letter was much longer than hers had been. He told her exactly what had happened and why the picture was in the glove compartment when she found it. He told her he would come home for the weekend as usual and if she wanted to see him, she should let him know.

I don't know if it will help, he thought as he folded the letter. *But the ball is in her court now. I've done what I can.*

He tensed every time the phone rang on Saturday. But none of the calls was for him. It was with mixed feelings that he attended church Sunday morning. The silence told him she had not changed her mind and they were finished. Would she be at church? She could hardly plead sick two Sundays in a row. What would she do if she was there? What should he do?

Miriam was already seated when John arrived. She took no notice of him, and he never saw her looking his way. When the service ended, he stayed with the other young fellows, but stationed himself so he could easily watch for her. He saw her coming with some other girls and took a hesitant step in her direction. His eyes, poignant with questions, sought for hers. She could not have helped seeing him, but swept by without giving him a glance, her head high and her cheeks aflame.

"Hey!" one of the fellows exclaimed. "Did you two have a fallout or something?"

"Or something," John answered shortly and turned on his heel to leave. He was humiliated by the public snubbing. He knew the news would spread like wildfire now.

"John and Miriam broke up . . . Did you hear the news? . . . I wonder why John and Miriam broke up . . ." Some might even say, "John's running around with girls in Allendale." If that report made the rounds, it would be because Miriam started it, he decided.

His initial humiliation turned into anger. *She doesn't believe me*, he thought bitterly as he spun out of the parking lot with a small shower of gravel. *She wouldn't even talk about it. All right then. It's over and I'm not sorry*, he thought with a savage sort of sadness. *I was getting awfully tired of babying her all the time. I wonder what I ever saw in her anyway. Any love I may have had for her is gone, too. We're both better off if we go our separate ways.*

Chapter 9

John wondered how his first week at Allendale could ever have dragged so slowly. *This* week seemed to fly. All week he toyed with the idea of staying in Allendale for the weekend. But by Friday evening he made up his mind. He would not be a coward and hide from any girl. He would just go home as usual and show Miriam he was not upset about their breaking up. He expected by now other people had heard about them through the grapevine, and he did not especially look forward to their remarks. But he would go to church as usual if for no other reason than to show Miriam he was quite happy without her.

Trying to act normal and as though nothing had happened was neither easy nor fun. It was actually hard work. It was obvious his and Miriam's breakup was common knowledge, and people wondered what had happened.

"John! Wait a minute," Becky called as he unlocked his car door to go home. He turned to see his sister hurrying toward him. She waved a flat paper bag. "I wanted to give you this. It's our gift to you for being in our wedding," she said as she handed the bag to him.

John took an 8 by 10 enlargement of Becky and Ken's bridal party from the bag and looked at it briefly. "That's pretty good," he commented.

"We were pleased with the pictures," Becky said. "I have some more in the car if you'd like to see them."

"Not today, thanks. I should go," John deferred. "I want to see them sometime though."

"Sometime when it won't hurt so much?" Becky hinted softly.

"Hurt? What do you mean?" He feigned innocency.

"I know you thought a lot of Miriam, and seeing pictures of yourselves together must not be easy for you," Becky explained unnecessarily.

"I *once* thought a lot of Miriam," he corrected. "But that's all over. We hadn't been getting along very well for quite awhile. It's true she did the breaking up, but I'm not sorry. If she hadn't done it now, I probably would have done it myself sooner or later. I'm not crushed and brokenhearted if that's what you think."

"Well . . ." Becky wavered, unsure of the right words, "I'm sorry anyway."

"Save your sympathy for someone that needs it," he retorted, grinning. "And thanks for the picture."

Becky stood silent, staring at the toe of her shoe. When she raised her eyes he saw she had not finished all she wanted to say. "John, I'm not sure how to say this, but may I just tell you one thing?"

"Sure. What's on your mind?"

"Just remember Samson. He would never have lost his life the way he did if he hadn't gone to the Philistines for a wife."

John guessed what she was implying. His eyes met hers and his defenses went up instantly. "And who said I've been visiting the Philistines?"

"Nobody, really. But they say they think that is why you and Miriam broke up. I wouldn't expect it of you," Becky hastened to say, "but I am worried about it. I'd hate to see you get mixed up with some girl."

"Were *they* plowing with my heifer, or did

they think that up all by themselves?" he scoffed. "*They* can say all they want to. It isn't true. I haven't been to the Philistines. So don't worry your pretty little head about it."

"I'm glad to hear that," she said with relief. "There is a nice wife somewhere for you. Keep looking and you'll find her."

So it's just as I thought, he mused angrily on the way home. *There's a lot of gossip going around about me. I wonder if there are any other churches that mind each other's business like the Mennonites. Why doesn't everybody just tend to their own affairs instead of gossiping about other people?*

The explanation he had given Becky for his and Miriam's breakup was the same one he had given his parents. They had accepted it without question though he knew they were a little disappointed. They had not imagined all sorts of wicked things about him. It made him wonder just how many details Miriam had told and to whom. His love for her had faded with the summer and died in the fall. His heart, like the fast-approaching winter, was now empty and void of any tender feelings for her.

Though it was nice to be with his family on weekends, John did not miss them as much as he had the first few weeks he had been away from home. In a way, it seemed sort of useless to make the long trip every weekend since he no longer had anyone special to see when he was there. He could not think of any other girl who interested him enough to begin dating. Again, he toyed with the idea of staying in Allendale for the weekend. He did not really feel like going home, and yet he did not know what he would do all weekend if he stayed. The decision was made for him on Friday.

"If this keeps up you might have to stay for the weekend," Joe said to John as they ate lunch. "It's early for a major snowstorm, but the forecast doesn't give much hope it will stop soon. You'll get your first taste of scraping snow tonight. And if it starts blowing the stuff, you can keep at it all day tomorrow, too."

"Oh well, I don't care as long as I get paid for it," John said.

"Overtime for anything after five and Saturday," Joe reminded him.

"Let it snow," John grinned.

When he called to let his family know he would not be coming home, his mother was surprised to hear how much snow they had in Allendale. There was only an inch of snow at home.

"I knew when I came I'd have to work when it snowed. So I guess this is one of those times. It just came a little earlier than we expected. I'll see you later," he promised before hanging up the phone.

The snow was the heavy, wet type and piled up quickly. But the storm blew over as unexpectedly as it had come. By Saturday noon the sidewalks and parking lot were cleared and the snow was already beginning to melt. His work finished, John had the rest of the day and Sunday to spend as he liked. He briefly considered going home after all, but quickly decided against it. It hardly seemed worthwhile to make the long round trip for one day at home.

"What are you doing tonight?" Sam asked John as the two hurried home across the parking lot.

"I don't know. Nothing special," John shrugged. "What are you doing?"

"I've got a date with Brenda. We're going roller skating at the rink. Wanna go along?"

"Me?" John laughed. "I'm not going to be a fifth wheel. Besides, I'd probably spend three-fourths of the time on the floor."

"I didn't mean for you to go without a partner. A good partner would hold you up, and I know where I could find one," Sam offered.

John considered. What *would* he do all weekend? Going along this evening would break the monotony. What harm could it do?

"Shall I ask her?" Sam's voice broke in on his thoughts.

"If you're thinking of Gwen, forget it," John dissented.

"No, not Gwen. This girl is more your type. And she's pretty, too. Come on. You don't have to worry about a girl at home anymore."

Why not? John thought, suddenly not caring. *If that's what people think of me anyway, I may as well go. It's only for one night. Just for something to do.*

"If she says yes, I'll go," he agreed.

"I'm sure she will say yes when I mention *your* name," Sam slapped him on the back. "You might as well have a little fun. You don't want to sit and rot all weekend."

John was foolishly pleased with Sam's approval. He enjoyed the evening more than he had expected he would. Marcella *was* pretty. John remembered seeing her working on third floor, though he had never taken any special interest in her. She was wholesome and friendly without being pushy or giddy. She really was "more his type," as Sam had said. They laughed together over John's frequent falls until he got the feel of the wheels under him and could stay on his feet. The touch of her small hand in his sent a stimulating tingle through his body. It was good to be with a girl who enjoyed his company. Though he had convinced himself he did not care about breaking up with Miriam, yet he had felt a twinge of disgrace that he had not been the one to end the relationship. His wounded ego was rapidly recovering tonight.

"I really enjoyed the evening," John told Marcella truthfully as he left her at the door of the nurses' residence. "Maybe we can do this again sometime."

"I'd like that," Marcella smiled. "Thanks for the nice time."

Now what was so bad about that? John thought as he crossed the parking lot to go to his room in the men's residence. *I don't feel a bit wicked. It didn't hurt a thing. Just because I went out with Marcella doesn't say I'm going to marry her. She is a nice girl, and we had some good, clean fun. That's all there was to it.*

Chapter 10

That one casual date with Marcella changed John's views of the girls he met daily in the hospital. New vistas opened which he had never seen before. As long as he had been dating Miriam, he had not encouraged the attentions of those who flirted with him, or like Gwen, chased him outright. Now he was flattered with their attention and found it easy to date them.

One girl led to another. They introduced John to new people and experiences. Weekends became a round of partying and fun. Eager to please and be accepted, he found himself doing things he never had intended to do. His spiritual roots had never been very deep. The slow spiritual deterioration he had been barely aware of now accelerated. Though he had not deliberately set out to follow this course, he slid rapidly into a downward spiral.

I can have a little fun without going too far, he told himself. *I can stop any time I want to.*

It was Joe who offered John the first cigarette he smoked. To Joe, smoking was as naturally a part of life as breathing. He shared his cigarettes like children share gum. John had always refused before when Joe offered him a smoke. Now he was tired of being an oddball. *Oh well, I've done other things, I may as well do this too*, he thought as he accepted Joe's offer and lit up.

As it had been with girls, so it was with smoking. One cigarette led to another. Before long he began to crave the taste of nicotine. The small packages his friends carried in their shirt pockets as part of their attire became part of his as well.

The clinking of glasses and ice at the bar was as much a part of the parties John attended with his new friends as was the blue smoke that hung above them. Social drinking was normal and abstinence abnormal. John was mortified to be abnormal and compromised by ordering a weak drink consisting mainly of ginger ale. He promised himself he would have only one drink at a party and that for social purposes only.

Never would he drink enough to become drunk.

The Fairlane he drove seemed terribly out of place among the sports cars his new friends drove. It was embarrassing to take a pretty girl out in such a "Mennonite car" that lacked even a radio. He traded the Fairlane in for a new red Mustang.

Life was flowing easily and smoothly along. John knew he was slipping fast and going further than he had intended to, but he was powerless to break out of the grip of the dizzying whirlpool into which he had fallen. *Oh well! Here I go!* he thought. As long as it felt good and he did not hurt anyone, it could not be too bad. He was enjoying life and having a good time. He did not want to stop long enough to think about how different he was rapidly becoming or do anything to disturb the pleasantness of life. Several times Mom wrote asking when he would come home again. She sensed all was not well and would have been appalled instead of simply alarmed had she known how rapidly he was rushing toward spiritual ruin. He answered her letters out of duty, but his answers were short and unrevealing. He pushed thoughts of home out of sight in the far corners of his mind.

Weeks stretched into months. He had not

been home since Christmas. He knew he should go, but the longer he put it off, the more he dreaded it. He had long ago decided never to be a hypocrite. If he went home now he would go as he was and not hide anything. He was not eager to reveal the changed person he knew he was. It was easier to stay away and avoid any conflict.

A letter from Becky at the beginning of April finally ended his procrastination.

"You haven't been home since Christmas," Becky wrote. "Won't you please come home for Easter next weekend? Pop doesn't say as much as Mom, but I know they are both worried about you. Mom cries a lot in church. It hurts me to see her so sad all the time. She is embarrassed when people ask about you and she doesn't know what to say. Please come home for her sake."

I may as well face the music, John thought. *I can't stay away forever.*

His appearance at home that Saturday morning caused a small furor. His younger brothers and sisters were greatly excited to see him drive in unannounced in a new car. It was more difficult than he had imagined to maintain a nonchalant manner. Though very little had changed at home, he felt a detachment from the family and their lives he had never sensed before. Everything seemed strangely old-fashioned.

Pop's pleasure at seeing John was shadowed by the significance of the small package in his shirt pocket and the sporty car. John read both messages in his face, though Pop said nothing on the latter. The twins had not forgotten him but regarded him with silent apprehension after the initial excitement had passed. He bribed them to sit on his knee, but they remained aloof. The younger boys dragged him all over the farm on a grand tour of their small world. He was a returning hero in their eyes. Mom's homemade chicken pot pie and the lemon meringue pie were unmistakably made in his honor. He enjoyed these favorites and appreciated her gesture, yet it made him feel more like company than ever. He realized he could no longer slip easily from one world to the other as he had once done. Still, it was nice to be home.

John knew his parents well enough to know they would not remain silent about his long absence or the changes they had seen. He was relieved when Becky and Ken came to visit Saturday evening and stayed until past the usual bedtime. Their presence helped him avoid an unpleasant confrontation. Marlin had a date, so John was left alone in his and Marlin's room.

On Sunday morning, John reached for a

shirt hanging on his side of the closet. His suit hung where he had left it the last time he had been home. He knew he would be expected to wear it, but did not feel right about putting it on. He had no right to wear the plain suit that symbolized his old life when his life now was not consistent with that. To put it on would make him the hypocrite he was determined not to be. He decided to wear a pale blue shirt and no suit coat at all.

At church, like at home, John felt like company. The Sunday school teacher of the youth class routinely asked one of the class to lead in prayer before beginning the class period. John tensed, fearful of being chosen, as he remembered this practice. His premonition was not mistaken.

"It's good to have you back with us again, John," the teacher smiled a welcome. "Would you lead us in prayer?"

John stumbled through what he hoped passed for a prayer. He was embarrassed at his own discomfort and clumsiness. Yet, he could not tactfully refuse to comply with the request. How long had it been since he had prayed privately, let alone publicly? He had no idea. He had never established a fixed pattern of private devotions at home though his father daily conducted family devotions.

The practice of praying before meals, which was part of eating at home, was never observed by John or those with whom he ate in Allendale. It could be no secret he was out of practice, though he had not realized it himself until now.

His mind wandered as the church service and sermon progressed. He had never made a practice of following closely though he usually had listened with at least half an ear. His thoughts were brought up short when one of Brother Gingrich's remarks jolted him to attention.

"There are those who say you can indulge in all kinds of perversions and satisfy your own fleshly appetites and surely you will not die. You can enjoy life a little and you're not going to die. Satan tries to present God as a liar. One of his tactics is distorting truth. And what he doesn't distort he holds up for ridicule. Eve knew exactly what God had said. But by listening to Satan's voice, she found herself slowly moving to a point where she was charmed. After that she was not prepared to combat the evil one. She had seen this tree before, but all of a sudden she saw it in a new way. She saw it was pleasant and desirable. Her mind was conditioned and prepared to fall away. She entertained thoughts that had never entered her mind before. First she looked, and then she took the fruit into her hands. At this point she was as close to sinning as she could be without actually sinning.

"Here is another step away from God. I see many professing Christians today who want to walk with the world and enjoy the things Satan has to offer. They walk as close as they can without actually sinning. I tell you, my dear people, that's dangerous! No one is strong enough to walk that close to forbidden fruit and withstand it. I say no one!

"Satan is a professional at making things look attractive. Cigarette advertisements show a healthy, rugged man with a lot of stamina, vigor, muscles, and color in his face taking a deep, long drag on a cigarette. How deceptive! Satan doesn't advertise what happens to a man that smokes. He doesn't show the emphysema, the hacking coughs every morning, or the cancerous lung. No, he tries to paint a picture that is not real.

"The same is true of liquor. We see liquor signs along the highway that have an attractive man and woman in a beautiful mountain scene, trying to show liquor for what it is not. Satan doesn't advertise what liquor does. He doesn't show a drunken bum on the street or the auto crashes with the blood and tangled metal. He doesn't tell that people who indulge in liquor have an ugly hangover the next morning. He tries to win people by their senses, painting a picture that is not real or true."

He's preaching at me! John thought angrily.

"Satan was right when he told Eve her eyes would be opened," the minister continued. "They surely were opened! Adam and Eve's eyes were opened in a way they never expected. They understood too late to turn the clock back. People who fall into sin hate themselves; they despise themselves and say 'If only, if only, if *only* I could turn the clock back.' But that is not possible. The clock cannot be turned back. This is what makes the horror of guilt so unbearable. People realize they did not have to do what they did. Yielding to doubt, charm, and temptation gives birth to shame, guilt, and fear.

"Adam and Eve did not know where to go to get away from God. Man doesn't think how he can avoid facing God when he is entertaining thoughts of sin in his life. God came seeking Adam and Eve, asking 'Where art thou?' He is asking you and me the same question. 'Where art thou? Where are you going?' He doesn't want to know which bush you are hiding behind. He knows that. He's asking where you are spiritually. If you were face to face with God this morning and He asked you that question, what would you say?"

I wonder who has been telling tales, John fumed to himself. *He doesn't need to pick on me the minute I step inside the door. He ought to preach on coveteousness, materialism, pride, and gossip. Let him preach at some of the old faithfuls that are so self-righteous.* John's ears were deaf to the rest of the sermon. He felt like leaving and never coming back.

Brother Gingrich shook John's hand and greeted him at the back of the church after the service had concluded. "Will you be back next Sunday?" he asked cordially.

"I'm not sure," John hedged untruthfully. He felt awkward and did not return the Christian greeting which he knew was expected.

"Next Sunday is our semiannual council meeting. You ought to be here if you can," the minister reminded.

John moved on without answering and went outside with the other young men. They were glad to see him and said so. "Where have you been all this time?" and "What have you been doing with yourself?"

were the two common greetings.

He answered lightly and noncommittally. *Nosey people!*

Somehow he did not feel like he belonged here, either. He had been away so long he had lost contact with the group and their activities—of who was engaged, who was going with whom, and who had broken up. He noticed Miriam left with Mervin Showalter. So she was going with him? Well! He was welcome to her. John could not have cared less. He headed home as soon as it was socially acceptable to do so.

"Do you want to go along to pass out *The Star* this afternoon?" Marlin asked as he pushed his chair in to the table after dinner.

"No, thanks," John refused. *Me? Pass out tracts? That's a laugh!*

"I told Jane I'd pick her up at 1:30, so I'll have to go right away," Marlin said for his parents' benefit. "Sure you don't want to go along, John?"

"I'm sure. Jane will be better company than I," John grinned.

"So they kept you busy this winter?" Pop said as Marlin left. Mom began clearing the table to wash dishes, and the rest of the family drifted out of the room.

"Sort of," John answered vaguely. *Here it comes!* he thought.

"We missed you," Mom said significantly.

"It *is* nice to be home again," John responded. "Except that Becky is gone, not much has changed."

"And how about you, John? Have you changed?" Pop asked. His tone was genuinely concerned.

"Do you think I have?" John avoided the question.

"I can see some changes," Pop said. "I'm wondering how deep they go. I don't mean to be nosey, but I am concerned that you don't lose your faith. Do you go to church when you don't come home?"

"No, I don't," John answered honestly. "There is no Mennonite church in Allendale, and I never hunted another kind."

"What do the other IWs do about church? Doesn't anybody bother?" Pop was incredulous.

"Some of the married couples take turns having church in their homes."

"And you never go?" Mom asked, disappointment showing.

John shook his head.

"Why not?"

"I don't know," he shrugged. "I guess I just never got started."

"Don't you think you should?" Pop suggested.

"I guess so," John allowed.

"Did you think about council next week and communion the week after that? Were you planning to come home for it?"

"I don't know." John's answer was evasive.

All three were silent. The conversation was failing to accomplish much in the way of communication.

"Doesn't any church oversee or give help to the IWs in Allendale?" Pop asked at last.

"There was a minister once. But he left and no one ever came to replace him."

"How many IWs are there now?"

"They come and go all the time," John said. "With the war in Vietnam escalating, they are coming faster than they are going. I'd say there are about 25 right now."

"I'm sorry we didn't choose a place more carefully," Pop said sadly. "Every place there are IWs should have a church and minister. We should not let our IWs adrift. But I guess it is hard for the church to keep pace with the rapid growth of the IWs in these past months. I wish you would have gone into VS instead. All the VS units have churches and houseparents."

"Is that Sam you work with still there?" Mom asked.

"Yes, but his time is almost up. He will be going home in two weeks," John said.

"He never sounded like the best company from what you said about him before," Mom remarked. "You're heading for a life of grief and heartache if you follow him."

"I'm not as bad as he," John objected.

"You haven't tried to hide from us that you have picked up the smoking habit," Mom said bluntly. "That tells me you are keeping bad company. And I wonder why you thought you had to get the kind of car you are driving. Oh, John! I'm afraid for you. Don't let yourself slip away. Surely there are some young men at Allendale who are keeping their faith. Stay away from those who are a bad influence, and make good friends that will help you," she pleaded.

"I guess I am headed the wrong way," John admitted. "But I can't help myself."

"None of us can help ourselves," Pop pointed out. "We need God's help."

John traced the pattern on the tablecloth with his finger. For the first time since he had begun drifting away he thought seriously about his way of life. He mentally compared the crowd he travelled with against the group who was passing out tracts that afternoon. There was no question which was a good or bad influence, and he knew it. Mom and Pop would be horrified if they knew some of the places he went and the things he did at Allendale.

"I wish we could take you out of there and start over at a better place," Pop said wistfully. "But the law prevents that."

"You can make a new start in your heart though," Mom suggested. "I'm sure it wouldn't be easy, but it *is* possible."

You have no idea how hard it would be, John thought. Yet, he had to admit his parents were right. He could not be as offended by their counsel as he had been by the sermon he had heard that morning. Their voices were alive with their love for him. How could he scorn his mother's pleading and his father's appeal?

"I'll try to do better," he promised. And in that moment he truly meant it.

Chapter 11

As his Mustang sped towards Allendale, John's good intentions evaporated.

I can't do it, he thought to himself. *I'd have to stay away from Sam, and I can't do that. We work together and everything. Maybe after Sam leaves I can turn over a new leaf. It will be easier then.*

So John returned to Allendale and his life there without changing anything. In his own heart he knew what he should do, but he was not willing to pay the price. If he did not think about the disappointment he was to his family, he was happy and comfortable with life just as it was. Telling himself he would make a change later salved his conscience.

Sam was not planning to stay on in Allendale after his two years of IW were completed. But neither did he want to go back to

Indiana. He could never be Amish again, he said. That would be much too tame after the life he was now used to. He decided to go to Florida for awhile and look around. Maybe he would like it there. He was free and unattached to anyone. He could come and go as he pleased.

The last Sunday night Sam was in Allendale, his friends had a farewell party for him. John never considered not going. He would miss Sam after he left. The place would never be the same without him. The party was like any other this crowd was used to having. John dismissed from his mind any thoughts of reform and threw himself into the party. His resolve to have only one drink at a party had long ago fallen by the wayside. He had been tipsy on several occasions, but never totally drunk. This night, he threw all caution to the winds. It was his last fling with Sam, perhaps forever.

By the time the party broke up in the wee hours of the morning, John was thoroughly drunk. He felt his way to his room, steadying himself against the wall as he went. Once in his room, he sat on the edge of the bed and tried to kick off his shoes. Suddenly, the room seemed to tilt at a crazy angle; his stomach wrenched and heaved. He lay weakly on the bed, letting his stomach empty itself of its contents. At last he lay quiet and still. Vaguely, he knew he should clean up the mess. But he must rest until he could stop trembling.

Light was streaming in the window when he awoke. He had no idea how long he had slept. He had a splitting headache and opened his eyes with a groan. His nose wrinkled in distaste before he was aware that the odor came from the bed in which he was lying. He sat up groggily and put his head in his hands. He was still fully dressed and coated with his own filth. The knowledge of what he had done shamed him. Trying to ignore the hammering in his temples, he peeled off his filthy clothes and rolled them in a bundle with the soiled bedclothes. He would just put everything in the garbage can and buy new ones, he decided as he headed for the shower.

He knew he was late, but he pulled himself together and reported for work anyway. He was surprised to find all of the maintenance personnel except Sam still in the supply room. By this time of the morning they were usually all scattered through the building and working at their various assignments. Through the fog of his hangover, he sensed something was amiss. The men stood in a cluster, talking in low tones. They turned half-pitying, half-questioning eyes on him and fell silent when he appeared in the doorway.

"What's wrong?" John's voice betrayed his ignorance and fear.

"Didn't you hear the news?" Joe asked.

"No. What news? What happened?" John fired questions in such rapid succession no one could answer between them. "Somebody tell me what's wrong!"

"It's Sam," Joe answered for the group. "He was in an accident early this morning on the way home from the party."

"What happened? Is he hurt?" the shocking news helped clear John's head.

"He's still alive," Joe answered the last question first. "They aren't sure if he'll live through the day. He has some internal and head injuries. There could be brain damage, but they don't know yet. He is just pretty well banged and beat up. He's in the ICU. Didn't you hear the ambulance come in?"

John shook his head numbly. He was so used to hearing the ambulance come and go he often did not hear it even when he was sober. "What happened?"

"Nobody knows for sure," Joe replied. "Sam and his girl must have gone somewhere after the party with Gwen and her guy. Nobody knows where they were. They were all stoned. Around 3:30 this morning they ran head on into another car. It was pretty messy."

"Was anybody—killed?" John asked hoarsely.

Joe nodded. "The guy in the other car. He was the father of four kids on his way home from the night shift."

"Too bad," John shook his head. "How are the others that were with Sam?"

"All dead, except Sam." Joe's voice sounded too loud in the quiet room. "Gwen and her guy were both dead on arrival, and Sam's girl died about an hour later. Sam was thrown out and that's what kept him from being crushed in the wreckage like the others. Gwen's guy was driving. He was crushed between the seat and the steering wheel. His legs were gone—ground like hamburger. None of them are very pretty to see. The car looks like a squashed beer can."

John was stunned and speechless. How could four lives, just like that, be gone? And Sam! Lying in the Intensive Care Unit of the hospital where he had worked just a few days less than two years. It couldn't be true. Yet, it must be. The faces of the men in the room told him it was no joke. A sudden urgency to see Sam seized him.

"I must go up and see Sam," he said in a shaking voice. "All right?"

"I doubt if they will let you in, but you can try," Joe consented. "Come back as soon as you can. We have to get to work."

"I'd like to see Sam Troyer," John requested permission at the nurses' station.

"Are you a relative?" the head nurse asked.

"No."

"I'm sorry. Visiting is permitted only by members of the immediate family."

"But I've *got* to see him." John was desperate. "He is my best friend. We both work here in maintenance."

"He is unconscious. He wouldn't know you. He's in critical condition."

"I won't say anything," John promised. "Just please let me see him."

The nurse seemed to be reconsidering. "All right," she said at last. "Since his family is out of state and you are his best friend, I'll let you in. But you may stay only a few minutes, and please do not disturb him. He is in the first bed on the right."

"Thank you." John's grateful voice was hushed. He ran the tip of his tongue nervously over his dry lips as he entered Sam's room.

If the nameplate on the head of the bed had not said "Samuel Troyer—Nothing By Mouth," John would never have recognized the still mound under the white sheet as his comrade. Joe's description of the violence of the crash had not prepared John for this sight. Sam was obviously only barely alive. A maze of wires and tubes connected him to various machines, monitors, and bags of life-giving solutions which slowly dripped through needles into his battered body.

John stood silent, staring at the too-white face. He must be having a horrible night-mare. Soon he would wake up and find Sam out in the hall somewhere, painting walls. This could not be Sam! The last John had seen him, Sam was having the time of his life at the party and talking of his plans for the week. All that was changed now. Sam would not leave for Florida on Thursday. If he left by Thursday, it would be through the doors of the morgue. John shuddered. He remembered too well the morgue in the basement and the silent, sheet-covered litters he had seen there. It gave him a spooky feeling to be in the morgue, and he always left as soon as he could.

They can't take Sam there! They just can't! John felt panic rising and he choked on a sob.

"You better go now," a nurse's soft voice whispered as her gentle fingers touched his sleeve.

John turned and looked numbly into the

face of the nurse beside him. It was one of the most attractive faces he had seen in the hospital. Her features were delicate and refined. Her full lips softly curved into finely finished little corners that hinted there would be dimples if they smiled. Her expression was sober, meditative, and sympathetic. He nodded wordlessly, only barely aware of her presence, and shuffled heavily from the room. Mechanically, he returned to the maintenance supply room.

Lynette Eisleman returned to the nurses' station and stood watching the retreating form of the man she had just sent away. "What do you know about that guy?" she asked the head nurse.

"He's John Shenk—from the maintenance department," Nancy Peters said. She had been at Allendale General for 25 years and was acquainted with many of the employees.

"I know that from his uniform and ID pin," Lynette said. "But what do you know *about* him?"

"He comes from some other state—Pennsylvania, Maryland, Virginia, or Ohio—I'm not sure. He's a IW."

"What do you mean, IW?"

"He's a Mennonite. They don't believe in going to war. So they serve two years in this kind of work instead of going into the army."

"Single?"

"Single. But don't get any ideas," she added swiftly. "You won't get him."

"You think so? Doesn't he take girls out?"

"Oh, yes. But he never gets serious with them."

"Humph! I never met a man yet I couldn't get if I wanted him."

Joe looked up when John returned. "How is he?"

"Terrible," John croaked. "I saw him. I don't feel like working. Could I have the day off?"

"Working might be the best thing for you," Joe advised. "But if you don't feel up to it, I suppose we can get along without you for one day. The work will keep."

John was not more than back in his room until he wished he had taken Joe's advice. He wished he had not seen Sam. Visions of that white face haunted him. He paced restlessly back and forth, not knowing what to do. He wanted to run, run, run and return to find everything back to normal. It was the longest day of his life. His own thoughts rose up like sea monsters to accuse him. He had no recollections of coming in the night before or of his drunken state. Yet, the evidence that morning had left no doubt of his condition the night before.

He could not understand why he had not been with Sam at the time of the accident. Usually, they went everywhere together. In vain he struggled to remember how he had gotten home. Why had he come home safely and not Sam? It was not because he was in any better condition than Sam after the party. He could be lying in ICU instead of Sam . . . or worse, in the morgue. He shuddered every time he thought of the morgue. He felt disgraced and dirty knowing how he had spent the night. He vowed to do better from now on. He would never again drink so much.

It was impossible to stay away from ICU. John felt compelled to go. He made several trips to the nurses' station for progress reports that day. There was no improvement, but when Sam's condition didn't worsen, John began to have a thread of hope.

Sam's parents arrived the next day. John met them in the ICU lounge where they kept vigil between the brief visits they were allowed every hour. They were grateful for John's concern and found a measure of comfort in talking to their son's best friend.

Every morning, noon, and evening, John checked with the nurses on Sam's condition. For several days the answer was always, "No change." On the noon of the fifth day, Sam's father met John as he stepped off the elevator. His face told John there was good news.

"Sam asked for water!" the elder Troyer reported with excitement. "He's coming around."

"Very good!" John joined in the rejoicing.

John's face had not only become familiar to all the ICU nurses by this time, but was also expected, since his visits were as regular as the clock. His steady, genuine interest in Sam and his parents earned the respect of all the nurses and he was on a first name basis with most of them. Lynette was especially interested in the earnest, faithful friend of her patient. She usually managed to be near Sam's bed when it was time for John's regular visits. The more John saw of her the more he was attracted to her. His visits to Sam soon were for a double purpose and seemed incomplete if she was not there.

"Did he ask you out yet?" Nancy asked as the double doors closed on John's back after one of his morning visits.

"Not yet. But he will," Lynette laughed. "He's nibbling the bait."

"He might take you out, but he won't get serious," Nancy warned.

"Wanna bet?" Lynette challenged. "I could go for this guy. He seems like a real gentleman, and his looks aren't bad either. I'll bet you a hundred bucks I can get him to marry me before Christmas."

"You're on," Nancy laughed shortly. "You'll never get that far so soon."

A determined gleam shone in Lynette's eyes. "Wait and see," she shot back.

Chapter 12

"Isn't this a coincidence!" John exclaimed lightheartedly as he entered the swinging double doors of the ICU and found Lynette standing just inside with the chart rack. "I was hoping to see you when I came up this morning. What's the good word?"

"Hello, John," Lynette smiled warmly. "We have good news and bad news this morning. Shall I tell you myself or let Sam tell you?"

"Don't keep me in suspense. Tell me the good news, but keep the bad," he matched his voice to the lilt in hers.

"Sam's being moved out of here this morning. That's the good news," she smiled.

"And what is the bad news?"

"I thought you didn't want to hear that," she teased.

"Oh, come on! I didn't mean that and you know it."

"If you insist, I'll have to tell you then. The bad news is—when Sam is moved out of here, you won't come up to see him anymore. We're so used to seeing you every day we'll miss it when you don't show up at the regular times."

"Is that all?" John laughed. "You know, I was going to tell you, I don't think we should go on meeting this way," he said in pretended conspiracy. "I'd like to see what you look like in a color other than white. Would you go out with me?"

"I might." She faked indecision.

"Are you free tomorrow evening?"

"The choir from Salem College is giving a concert at my church tomorrow evening. You're welcome to go with me if you'd like," she said.

"Sounds interesting. What time should I come for you?"

"If you come at 6:30 we should have plenty of time to get to the church," she said.

"Fine," he agreed. "Now I better run on in to Sam before he wonders what happened to me. See you then," he waved as he turned to go.

He was not aware of the triumphant look on Lynette's face as he strode toward Sam's room. He was on her hook! Now, if she could just make the right moves, she could win her bet and land her man.

John was intrigued with Lynette. Her pretty face and friendly, reserved manner set her apart from other girls he had dated here. He thought she was different without knowing why. So she was a Christian! That was even more interesting and probably explained the difference in her. Frankly, he was getting a little bored with the way he was living. It was not as thrilling as it had been at first. The company of a Christian girl might be the refreshing change he needed. He had a feeling she could turn out to be even better than he had thought.

After the first signs of returning consciousness, Sam's progress had been painful and slow, but sure. The news that he had made sufficient improvement so the constant monitoring was no longer necessary was welcome. It seemed certain now Sam would live, although it was too soon to tell if he would have any permanent damage. His parents reluctantly returned home to attend to their home duties when his life was no longer in doubt. They were kept posted on his condition and promised to return when he was ready to be released.

The three daily visits John had made while

Sam was in ICU were now reduced to one at the end of the work day. It was good to see Sam sit up and talk normally again, though his voice was soft and weak. He was beginning to look more like himself again in spite of an obvious loss of weight and color.

"How's it going today, old man?" John grinned as he poked his head in Sam's door one evening a few weeks later.

"Slow, but sure," Sam responded. "They had me down in therapy today learning to walk. Whew! I never would have believed it could take so much effort to walk a couple of feet between two bars. But they said I did great and all I need is practice and exercise. I've been lying here in bed so long my muscles are all flabby and useless. But I can be thankful there is no paralysis."

"Sounds great." John clapped an encouraging hand on Sam's shoulder. "You'll be out of here and chasing girls again in no time."

Sam's face clouded. "I've been thinking about that lately, John. In fact, I've been thinking about a lot of things since I have all this time on my hands. I'm not much at making speeches of this sort, but . . . well . . . it's like this. I know I haven't lived right while I was here in IW. I guess I thought I could do as I pleased away from home and nobody would know. I forgot that God saw everything. He finally brought me to my senses, and I confessed my sin to Him. But it cost four lives and very nearly my own. I am so ashamed of the way I lived." Tears coursed down his cheeks.

"I wrote a letter to my parents and asked them to forgive me," he went on when he could speak again. "When I get out of here, I am going back to Indiana to my parents and my church."

John was speechless at this unexpected announcement.

"I want to tell you how sorry I am for taking you with me down the wrong road," Sam continued. "Don't keep on. You were taught what is right. If you keep on the way I led you, you might end up like I did—or almost did. I would never forgive myself if that happened."

"Look, Sam, I'll admit I've changed since I've been in IW. But don't blame yourself for that. I didn't do anything I didn't want to do," John tried to soothe his troubled friend.

"But I was the one who encouraged you to be like I was," Sam lamented. "I started you playing cards, dating girls, and drinking. Such a fool I was! If you ever listened to me before, listen to me now. Give up all those things and go back to your church."

"If it makes you feel any better, I am

turning over a new leaf," John confessed. "To be honest, I guess your accident has made me think. To this day I don't know why I wasn't with you that night. I was drunk and don't remember how I got home. I decided then I'd never drink so much again, and I've only had a few since."

"It won't work," Sam shook his head. "Just turning over a new leaf isn't the answer. I tried that myself a couple of times. You can't do it yourself. You need help, God's help."

"Lynette is a Christian. I am going to church with her. And you know, I enjoy it more than I thought I would. It is kind of nice for a change to be with a different crowd. I don't have to be a Mennonite to be a Christian, do I?"

"No," Sam admitted. "But be sure you know what you are doing so you don't get in a mess like I did. You really think a lot of Lynette, don't you?"

"More than any girl I ever dated here," John said emphatically. "She's different and—well—sort of wholesome. I enjoy being with her, and we have good times."

"What would your parents think of her?" Sam prodded.

"Hey! I've only learned to know her. I'm not that far yet," John laughed dryly.

"You ought to take it into consideration,"

123

Sam said seriously.

"She's a lot better than the girls you took out," John was annoyed. "Stick to your own reformation, and I'll take care of myself. I'm a big boy now."

"It's not reformation we need; it's transformation," Sam said softly. "Be transformed by the renewing of your mind—"

"Yeah? Well, I'd better go get my supper before the cafeteria closes," John stood up abruptly. "See you later."

He must have some brain damage, John mused as he headed for the cafeteria. *He used to like to call himself "wild and wooly, big unruly me." Now he's starting to sound like a preacher, and an Amish one at that! It won't last. When he is out of this hospital he'll soon be the same old Sam. I guess we did go a little too far sometimes, but I'm doing better now. He can go back to his church if he wants to, but I'm not ready to do that. There are too many hypocrites in the church. If I go to any church it will be because I want to and believe in it for myself; not because somebody told me that is what is right.*

When Sam was finally released from the hospital nearly three months after the accident, no one was more surprised than John at the total change that had occurred in the former flamboyant playboy. Sam read his Bible and put on his Amish clothes without embarrassment. He was genuinely eager to go home to Indiana with his parents when they came for him.

He really must mean it after all, John finally concluded. *I can hardly believe how different he is. But it's a free country, and if that is what he wants, it's all right with me.*

Chapter 13

"What I wouldn't give for some good home cooking!" John sighed as he slid his tray onto the table at lunch time. "This stuff is edible, but it sure gets monotonous after awhile."

"I know what you mean," Lynette agreed as she slid into the seat opposite him. She had begun meeting him for lunch when her schedule allowed it. "I was just telling my mom how tired I would get of this food if I were you. She said she'd be glad to have you come for lunch on Sunday. Why don't you come to church with me and then stay for lunch? My family is dying to meet you."

"I'm really tempted." He toyed with his fork. "But I don't know about meeting your family."

"Don't be silly," she laughed. "My kid

brothers will adore you. Apple cake is Mom's specialty."

"I could never turn that down with this in front of me," he wrinkled his nose at the tasteless meal on his tray. "I'll be there."

The Sunday with the Eislemans was the most enjoyable time John had had in a long time. Their house, set on a large lot in a quiet, fashionable section of town, was comfortably furnished and tastefully decorated without being overly elaborate. Lynette's parents did not attend the morning worship with the young couple, but warmly welcomed John to share their noon meal when the two returned from the service. There was a satisfying feeling in going to church and being part of a family around the dinner table afterward. Until now, he had not realized how much he missed the stability and sense of belonging that was missing in his way of life.

While Lynette helped her mother clear the table after the meal, John pitched a few balls for her brothers on the lawn.

"It's been a long time since I played ball," John rubbed his arm when he finally dropped to the grass beside Lynette. "I didn't know my pitching arm was in such bad shape."

"You'll have to do this some more then,"

she smiled into his eyes.

"You'll probably have to bar the door to keep me out after this," he teased. "I don't know when I have enjoyed a day so much for a long time."

"Consider this a standing invitation," she said, giving his hand an affectionate squeeze. "My folks may be hard to please, but you passed inspection with flying colors. You made a hit with my brothers, too."

"You know, I guess I miss my family more than I realized." He was serious now. "Being with your family today made me realize how lonely my life is. I'm not really alone; there are other guys in the same building. But one room isn't really what you could call a home. And the other guys aren't the same as a family. It's worse than ever now with Sam gone."

"Tell me about your family," she encouraged. "You never said much about them, and I am curious."

John described his family, telling little things about each one.

"They all sound so interesting!" she exclaimed in fascination when he finished. "Your little sisters must be dears."

"Maybe I'll take you to meet them some day," he said, picking up her hand and absently playing with her slim fingers.

"Would you?" She gave an excited little gasp. "I'd love to meet them. But maybe they wouldn't like me."

"Now who is being silly?" he teased, giving her a playful shake. "My family is different from yours, that's true. But they can't help but like you when they see you. You are the nicest girl I ever knew."

Lynette kept her eyes lowered modestly to hide the gleam of satisfaction in them. He was going even faster than she had hoped.

"Why, Mr. Shenk! What a flatterer you are!" She jumped to her feet and held out her hand invitingly. "Let's get out of this sun. I think it is affecting you."

Their romance escalated rapidly. It was plain to see he was smitten with her and she adored him. Her demure responses to his advances only increased his desire for her. She was such a pleasant, comfortable person to spend a day with—or a lifetime. A longing to belong seized him, to belong to a family, to belong to Lynette.

His weekends were usually free, but she often had to work. Whenever she had a Sunday off, he took advantage of the standing invitation for lunch with her family. They always welcomed him warmly and made no attempt to hide their pleasure at his interest in Lynette.

"Dad is taking his vacation next week," Lynette told John over their lunch in the cafeteria one day. "They will be leaving Saturday for a whole week at the ocean. Sure wish I could go, too," she sighed. "But it's out of the question."

"It would be nice to get away from this heat for awhile," he agreed mildly. "But I guess we can't expect anything else this time of year."

"We can't go to the ocean for a week, but maybe we could escape for a day. I was just thinking this morning . . . I could pack a picnic lunch, and we could spend Sunday out at the lake. How would that sound?" she asked.

"Great!" he enthused.

"It wouldn't be as good as a week at the ocean, but it will have to do. It's all we can manage," she said.

"I suppose you want to go to church first?" There was a question in his voice.

"Oh, let's skip it this time." She waved the question aside. "I can use a whole day of rest for a change. It will be wonderful."

"Whatever you say." He would agree to do whatever she wished.

It was a wonderful day, just as she had predicted. The tall, spreading trees near the lake formed a natural canopy of protection from the scorching heat of the sun as they picnicked in the shade. John lavishly complimented Lynette on the lunch she had packed. She accepted the praise modestly, seeing no need to confess it had been purchased at the Deli.

They swam in the lake and strolled along the beach.

The day passed pleasantly and swiftly. They were two people in complete agreement. It seemed there was no time, no place, nothing other than the two of them in the world. They capped the day with a leisurely meal in a small cafe on the way home.

"It's been a wonderful day," she sighed as she handed him the key to unlock the door. "I hate for it to end. Won't you come in awhile? I'll get you some Scotch—or whatever you like—from Dad's bar." Her voice was like a child's.

He smiled. "I hoped you would ask." His conscience, pleasantly lulled to sleep, voiced neither objection nor warning as he followed her into the deserted house and closed the door behind him.

Chapter 14

When John asked Lynette if she would like to go home with him to meet his family, she was eager to go. At his suggestion, she had worn the most subdued dress she owned. He well knew what his parents' reaction would be to a girl in slacks. And Lynette, anxious to make a good impression, was willing to comply. She knew she would have to work extra hard to gain the approval of John's family since she was so different from them. Yet, she looked forward to the meeting with anticipation, not dread. It would be a novelty to spend a day in a Mennonite home.

The Shenks were still in church when John and Lynette arrived at the farm. While they waited for the family to return,. he showed her around the farm. She exclaimed

132

over a nest of kittens in the barn and was delighted with the fragrance of the haymow. They walked, hand in hand, through the meadow to the old crab apple tree where he had once built a tree house. She laughed at the mental image of him as a country boy in bib overalls with a straw in his teeth, lying on his stomach on the platform in the tree and listening to the gurgling of the stream below. It seemed almost funny to him, too— as if it had happened to someone else long ago.

When the family car finally came in the lane, with Ken and Becky's following close behind, she turned eagerly to watch them coming. She did not seem to notice the slightly awkward and hesitant way in which he introduced her to his family. She responded in such a friendly way the momentary strain was set aside. She insisted on helping to put the noon meal on the table and cleaning up afterward, chatting pleasantly all the while. She complemented Ida on her cooking and copied a dessert recipe. In a sisterly way, Lynette inquired about Becky's health, since it was obvious she would be a mother in a few months. Babies were the sweetest, dearest things Lynette could imagine.

Jimmy and Carl maintained a noncommittal attitude toward their big brother's friend, but the twins gradually warmed enough to begin talking. Eventually, Lynette won their confidence and sat with one on each side, reading a story from a book they brought to her.

At Lynette's insistence, John showed her the whole house, even to the cellar with its rows of filled fruit and vegetable jars. She was amazed at the amount of food stored there and the work it must have been to preserve it. He took her upstairs to see the room where he had slept as a boy. She wanted to learn all about him.

While she stepped into the bathroom before starting back to Allendale, he started down the stairs. But he stopped on the landing at the turn in the stairs when he heard his mother speaking.

"She seems like a nice girl," Mom was saying. "But I don't see how she can be the Lord's perfect will for him. Can't you talk to him and stop him before he makes a mistake?"

"He is 21," Pop replied. "I can't make his choices for him. He knows what we have taught him. If we didn't get our point across to him before this, I'm afraid it's too late now. Still, I couldn't live with myself if I let him go without saying anything."

Momentarily, John was smitten with guilt. He knew without being told that Lynette was not what his parents would have preferred. But Mom had said she was a nice girl. They would soon learn to love her as he did, he was sure.

Less than two weeks later, Ida took the mail from the box, sifting through the junk mail to the few worthwhile pieces. She stopped short when she recognized John's handwriting on an envelope with a West Virginia postmark. He rarely took the time to write a letter home, and she certainly did not expect one so soon after his recent visit. With a woman's intuition, she suddenly guessed what the letter said.

Slowly, she walked in the lane and sank into a chair at the kitchen table. With shaking hands she drew a hairpin from her hair and slit the envelope carefully along its top edge. She drew the single sheet from the envelope and laid it on the table without unfolding it. She did not want to know what it said—and then she did. Perhaps she was just jumping to conclusions. She picked up the paper and shook it open.

Dear Pop and Mom, (she read)

I want you to know Lynette and I are planning to be married soon. We haven't set a date yet, but it will be

soon. You seemed to like Lynette
when you met her. I love her very
much. I am sure we will be happy
together. I will let you know more
about the wedding when we make
more plans.

Ida read no further. She bowed her head
on her folded hands above the letter. Her
heart was heavy with the choice her son was
making. How could her son, the one she had
loved and cared for so tenderly in the innocence of his babyhood and boyhood, so
quickly have become a man and left behind
all she had taught him? Was he marrying this
girl because he wanted to, or—the thought
took her breath away—because he *had* to?
She scanned the short note again. She could
not tell. In agony, she poured out to God all
the longings of her heart for the soul of her
wayward son.

She was not aware how long she sat at the
table, weeping and praying over the letter.
Slowly, the first overwhelming sense of disappointment and failure she felt, was replaced with a measure of the peace of God.
When Norman came in, she was able to tell
him the news without bursting into tears.

The next week Norman and Ida took time
on a busy weekday to visit John. They took
their minister and his wife with them. As

soon as John saw them, he knew why they had come. He listened politely to all they had to say but would not change his decision to marry Lynette. He could not bring himself to tell them the reason the wedding was taking place on such short notice. Time would explain it for him. It was too late to change what was done. Marrying Lynette was the only honorable thing he could do now.

When the four visitors left to return home, they knew it would take more than their words to change John's mind and direction. He could ignore their advice and pleadings, but he could not keep them from praying for him. Daily, their prayers ascended to the throne beseeching God to speak to this wayward son and bring him to repentance. He could reject his parents, his church, and his God. He could withdraw from them and shut himself away in a tight little circle that had no room for them. But he could not remove himself from the circle of their love. Wherever he went and whatever he did, their prayers and love would follow and surround him.

The wedding day was only six weeks away. Lynette had much to accomplish in a short time. She insisted on a big church wedding with all the fanfare. She gloated over gifts from a hastily arranged shower and the wedding gifts as they began to arrive. John rode along, feeling more like a spectator than a participant. He left all the wedding plans to her and her mother and agreed to whatever they suggested. But when Lynette made an appointment to have him fitted for a rented tuxedo, he balked.

"I can't wear such a get-up. I'd feel like a stuffed shirt," he protested.

She laughed. "Just like a man! What did you think you would wear?"

"Oh, I don't know. Just a regular suit, I guess."

"Mercy, no! This is a formal affair. All the wedding etiquette books say you must wear a tux for the kind of wedding we are having."

"Why must we have all this ado?" he groaned. "We could go to the preacher and get it over without all this fuss."

"You can't mean that," she cried. "Every girl wants a wedding to remember."

"Couldn't we keep it a little more simple?" he suggested.

"It's too late for that now," she said stubbornly. "Everything is ordered and it's too late to cancel. Come on!" Her tone changed to one of supplication. "You can stand a tux for one day, can't you? For me?"

He sighed. "Might as well be hung for a

sheep as for a lamb, I guess. I wouldn't do it for anyone else but you, and so help me, I never will again."

"You are a dear." She rumpled his hair affectionately. "And I love you."

John grinned foolishly and changed the subject. "Let's go look for an apartment tomorrow. I found one not too far from the hospital that I thought might be all right. But I want you to see it first. It's on Park Avenue."

"What is it like?" she asked.

"It has three rooms and a bath. The rent is $80 a month."

"Sounds all right to me. That's your department. I'll plan the wedding, and you find a place to live. I don't care where it is, as long as you are there," she said dreamily.

"But don't you want to see it?"

"If you want me to. But I know it will be fine."

John was a little surprised at her nonchalance about their first home. It was true, the apartment was only temporary, but he thought all brides-to-be were excited about setting up housekeeping. He supposed she was too busy with wedding plans just now to think about the domestic side of married life. That would come in its own time.

John rented the furnished apartment and

moved into it. Lynette often spent the night there with him. She said it was more convenient to go to work from there the next day than if she went home. Her parents made no objections since the wedding date was so near. John knew he and Lynette would be very happy together here in their first home. He was looking forward to the wedding and married life.

Chapter 15

"Nervous?" the best man questioned as he parked his car at the old stone church.

"A little," John replied with a stiff smile. He barely knew this person who was to be his best man. Lynette had chosen all eight of the attendants from among her friends. He could not ask anyone from home to be in his bridal party. Sam was out of the question, and he had no other close friends he wanted to ask. So he had left all the arrangements, including the choosing of the attendants, to Lynette.

"I've got the ring," the best man said, patting his pocket. "You don't have to worry about a thing."

The two of them entered a side door where they would wait for the proper time to enter the sanctuary. The wait seemed interminably long. He had not been allowed to see Lynette all day. He pictured her coming down the aisle and grew impatient. He could hear faint organ music, hushed and solemn. He had little idea of what was being played. He took his place at the head of the line of men, waiting to enter the sanctuary. At last, the signal was given. As he opened the door, a burst of music filled his senses. Soft candlelight, palms, flowers, and beautiful garments bewildered him. Instinctively, he shrank from the thought of going in to face the waiting guests.

But now the door was wide open, the organ swelling grandly. He was aware of many eyes. He swallowed and took his first step to the music. He walked with feet that suddenly weighed like lead, across a church that seemed to be miles wide, in the face of swarms of eyes. Most of them were strangers to him. He glanced furtively over the faces near the front. There was Lynette's mother, looking flushed but tranquil. His parents were seated across the aisle. His brothers and sisters were all there, as well as Marlin's Jane. Becky, heavy with child, sat with Ken behind her parents.

Was it just a year ago he had been best man at Becky and Ken's wedding? It seemed eons ago. Then, he had worn a plain suit, though somewhat self-consciously. Now, here he was in this ridiculous get-up Lynette had rented. He glanced back to his mother. She was wiping away a tear with a trembling hand. Beside her, his father sat straight, solemn, and pale.

The music stole onward. The bridesmaids, waiting in the vestibule, slowly and gracefully inched down the aisle. He could see Lynette with her hand on her father's arm, waiting their turn. Her father, pale and rigid, looked as though he would not be able to start down the aisle without a push from behind. But then, eight beats behind the maid of honor, Lynette and her father got started and were coming as the organ peeled the joyous notes of the wedding march from Lohengrin. The congregation began to rise. The maid of honor took her place and joined the others watching the father and daughter moving down the aisle.

They were near enough now that John could see Lynette smiling at him through her white illusion veil that fell from a crown of seed pearls and sequins. Her gown, of white silk organza over taffeta, rustled softly with each step. She carried a cascade of white roses and orchids.

The organ hushed its voice to a whisper and the minister, in a voice both impressive and musical, began the ceremony.

"Dearly beloved, we are gathered together . . ."

He seemed to be speaking the words as if
they had just been created for John and
Lynette. They were beautiful, old-fashioned
words, but it seemed to John he was hearing
them for the first time. Lynette's father gave
his daughter in marriage and took his seat
beside his wife.

The minister began to pray. Under cover
of the hush and supposedly bowed heads,
John stole a look at his bride. His heart
swelled with emotion. She was lovely. Her
head drooped and long lashes touched her
cheeks. He looked at her with such intensity
that she became aware of his gaze and raised
her eyes. They were brimming with tears.

All the experiences of their whirlwind
courtship and brief engagement rushed over
him. The tears in her eyes frightened him.
Was she marrying him against her will?
What had he done to her? What was he
doing now to her and to himself? When the
prayer ended, he was trembling.

A soft rustle of the audience and a little
breath of relief from the bridal party signaled
the next stage of the ceremony. The maid of
honor took Lynette's flowers. John and
Lynette stepped forward. Standing there, a

little apart from the rest of the bridal party, he realized with a start that they were being *married*. He was being joined to Lynette now for life. It was not a dream or a play they were acting out. It was real and for the rest of their lives. Shaking, he mechanically repeated the minister's words, taking vows upon himself that bound him to Lynette. The thing had passed from an adventure of the moment into awesome reality. But what else could he do? He really had no choice. He was the father of her child.

The best man produced a ring and nudged John. Lynette's hand, slender and white, was outstretched in front of him, the ring finger held away from the others. He slipped the gold circlet on her finger. She placed her hand in his. As his fingers closed over her hand there was such a tenderness in his touch that her eyes raised again to his. The tears were joined by an unspoken appeal. Involuntarily, he pressed her hand as if to give her assurance and strength. The procedure was reversed now, and Lynette slipped a gold band on his finger.

The ceremony was going much too quickly. There was no time to think. Something so solemn and binding should last longer.

And with that thought came the words, "I

pronounce you husband and wife. What God hath joined together, let no man put asunder."

Lynette's veil was thrown back to uncover her face. John kissed his wife and she retrieved her flowers from the maid of honor. The benediction was pronounced. With the last word, the swell of the organ filled the church. The audience stirred in anticipation of a full view of the wedding procession. Lynette placed her hand lightly on John's arm. They turned and fairly flew up the aisle.

Out in the vacant vestibule, they were alone together for a moment. It was over! They were married. *Married!* She was his! The thought brought a thrill of wonder to his heart. His love for her swept away all doubts. He knew he could take her to his heart, cherish her, love her, and bear with her for life.

Suddenly they were surrounded by their families. The guests were coming out of the sanctuary. The bridal party formed into a receiving line. Lynette was kissed and admired by men and women alike.

"A beautiful wedding . . . such a nice couple . . . a lovely bride . . ."

There was laughter and kissing everywhere. John felt sorry for his family. They were conspicuously out of place. He knew the corsage his mother wore had been accepted only because she had not known how to graciously refuse it. He knew she felt awkward with such an ornament, and it did not become her. He felt sorry for her, but did not know what to do about it. He was helplessly trapped in the situation.

They entered the reception room for the catered meal Lynette's parents had provided. The photographer followed the bridal pair's every move, taking scores of pictures for their wedding album. They cut the wedding cake and posed for more pictures. John hoped his parents would leave before the dancing began. As the orchestra began to tune up, he was relieved to see them preparing to go. He crossed the room alone to say good-by to them.

"You're going?" he asked unnecessarily.

"Yes," Pop answered, clearing his throat self-consciously. "Come home sometimes. Our door will always be open."

"Thank-you. We'll be there sometime," John promised, shaking hands awkwardly. He took his mother's hand. "Good-by, Mom. Have a safe trip home."

"Good-by, John," she whispered. Her eyes were round circles full of meaning and a love he knew he could never shake off. "God

147

bless you. We are praying for you both."

Without meaning to, her words had punctured the bubble of his happiness. He knew he had hurt his mother deeply with his marriage and he regretted that. He was glad when he and Lynette could leave through a shower of rice and confetti. The festivities were hollow somehow, and he felt a restlessness he could not define.

"I'm glad that's all over!" John let out his breath in a gush as they headed away from the noise of the dancing and celebrating that would continue until the early morning hours. "All that fuss and feathers isn't for me."

"Just like a man, again! I told you every girl wants a big wedding. The more guests, the more loot," Lynette laughed.

"Anyway—I saw Nancy Peters give you something just as we were about to leave. May I ask what it was?" He was curious.

"You may ask." Lynette's laugh bubbled. "It was a check for $100. Speaking of loot, how's that for a wedding gift?"

"A hundred dollars!" He was astonished. "Why would she give you such a big wedding gift?"

Lynette laughed and shrugged again. "Just a generous old soul, I guess. But it was sweet of her, anyway."

Chapter 16

The newlyweds spent a week in the warm Florida sunshine. They strolled through Cypress Gardens and rode the glass-bottomed boat at Silver Springs. They toasted themselves lazily on the beach, built a sandcastle, and collected pretty shells and driftwood. They dined at exclusive restaurants and slept in stylish motels. It was a pleasant life of freedom and ease. They wished it could go on forever. But all too soon it was time to return to Allendale and go back to the process of living and making a living.

Lynette went back to work the day after they returned from their honeymoon. Her hours were not as regular as John's. She often worked when he had off and vice versa. If they were both home at the same time, she usually opened tin cans or made TV dinners. She was busy writing thank-you notes for the wedding gifts and setting up housekeeping in their tiny apartment. The home cooking and quiet evenings together he had looked forward to did not develop. But he was sure that would come after they were settled. The little apartment was a cozy bridal nest. They were completely happy. John fully expected life to continue to be full of sunshine and pleasure.

Sleet drove into his face in sharp stabs as he walked to work one morning after several weeks of wedded bliss. His head was bowed against the force of the wind, his hands shoved deep into his pockets. He felt as if he carried the weight of the world on his shoulders. He had learned that Lynette had deceived him; tricked him into marrying her. After the first shock of disbelief and then the fierce heat of his anger had passed, icy fingers had gripped his heart, squeezing it dry of all feeling and leaving it cold, hard, and numb.

Silently, he cursed himself. How could he have been so stupid? Why had he taken her word without question? In a way, it was a relief to know he would not have to try to cover up or explain away a "premature" birth. There would be no birth at all. He was glad now he had not mentioned anything about it to anyone.

What have I done? What kind of woman have I married? he asked himself. *I never thought she would lie to me.*

In his blaze of anger, bitter words had been exchanged. He had seen a side of his wife's character he never knew existed. He really had known very little about her, he realized now. Today, she seemed like a total stranger. He had been tricked and he knew it. It was like being pulled from a delicious nap and plunged into an icy bath. He had made vows which could not be broken, regardless of the circumstances in which he had made them. He could not go back and undo what he had done. He would have to go on and make the best of it.

Lynette had known he would eventually learn the truth. She had expected a scene, but had not been prepared for the fury of his anger. He had always seemed calm and easygoing. He had not become violent, but she knew he was infuriated. She was afraid. She had thought he would brush it off with some light remark, saying he would have married her anyway. She knew now she had been wrong. It was she who had shattered their happiness, and it was she who would have to repair it.

She called in sick at work and took the

whole day planning how to appease her husband when he came home. He had given her enough hints that she knew he liked a tidy house and made-from-scratch meals. She spent hours poring over the cookbook and preparing the most elaborate meal she had ever cooked. The house was tidy and the table carefully set before he came home. As she worked, she wondered if she should act cool, hurt, repentant, or as if nothing had happened. Her answer came in an unexpected way when the mail arrived. The letter was addressed to Mr. and Mrs. John Shenk, so she did not feel guilty reading it though she knew it was from John's parents. It was an invitation to have Christmas dinner with his family. Lynette smiled to herself. She would apologize and then give him the letter. He was sure to cheer up when he thought of going home for Christmas. He could not stay angry forever. She was sure he would get over it.

The shining apartment and good meal were an obvious attempt to apologize, and John both recognized and accepted the offer. He wished he had not said some of the things he had, but felt justified because of her deceit. She was so contrite and loving now he could almost forgive her. She told him she was afraid some other girl would come along and take him from her. She convinced him she had loved him so much that even though she knew she should not do it, she had taken matters into her own hands. She could simply not wait to be his wife.

When they finally retired for the night, a truce had been called. John was still hurt, but the bitterness and anger had softened. He was committed to living with the choice he had made. She thought her day had been well-spent.

The approaching Christmas holidays made Lynette's job of keeping John happy much easier. She persuaded her family to arrange their festivities so as not to interfere with plans to visit John's family.

Together, they shopped for gifts for their families. The gifts she chose for her family were much more expensive than the ones he chose for his family. He complained good naturedly that she would send him to the poorhouse with her extravagance. She only laughed and called him Scrooge. She thought his gifts were cheap and too ordinary, but she let him buy what he pleased. He was glad to go home for Christmas, and she was pleased to see him happy. He was making a splendid recovery. Everything would soon be back to normal.

The weather cooperated with their plans.

Lynette snuggled close to him as they got into the cold car to start for his home. "Br-r-r-r, it's cold. But at least it isn't snowing," she remarked lightly.

"I should have warmed the car. Sorry," he apologized.

"It will soon be warm," she brushed his apology aside. "Our dream house will have a garage. We'll just rough it until then."

Christmas at home was the best tonic John could have taken for his wounded dignity. The calm peace of his family's Christmas customs was in sharp contrast to the festivities commonly associated with the world's way of celebrating. It was much more satisfying, really, than all the parties they had attended at Allendale.

"Best meal I've eaten in a long time," John complimented his mother after the delicious meal. "There's just nothing like Mom's home cooking."

"I'm glad you enjoyed it," Mom replied modestly. "That is what makes cooking worth the effort."

Lynette pretended she had not heard John's remark, but it annoyed her. Was he trying to tell his family she did not know how to cook?

The afternoon passed pleasantly with visiting, opening the gifts, and a family sing of old and new carols. Lynette was surprised to find there was no Christmas tree and that the simple gifts she feared would look cheap were the only kind exchanged. She was glad she had let John do the choosing and not insisted on the more elaborate gifts she had thought would be more suitable. She felt like an outsider in this circle. Their ways were vastly different from the life she had always known. She looked at Jane, beside Marlin, and wondered if John had ever had a sweetheart among his own people. Did he wish he had not married her? Would he want to go back to his old ways some day? Suppose he would want to be a Mennonite again. Would he want her to be one, too? Horrors! She would never dress like these women!

Becky and Ken's new baby girl was the day's main attraction. Less than three weeks old, she was passed from lap to lap all day. The small twin aunts actually fought over who would hold her and for how long.

"You girls have been so selfish with this baby, Lynette hasn't had a turn to hold her yet," the new grandma said. She settled their disagreement by giving the precious bundle to Lynette.

Lynette took the child that was put into her arms. She was afraid to look at John beside her until he reached for the baby's hand. She grasped the finger and waved her other tiny fist.

"She's saying, 'Hi, uncle,'" Lynette laughed.

"This is when cows are a nuisance," Pop said, standing and stretching. "They don't even let us off for Christmas. But if we're going to get to church on time, we have to go get started on the chores. Come along, boys."

Jimmy and Carl reluctantly changed into old clothes and followed their father to the barn.

"What is at church tonight?" Lynette whispered to John under cover of the hubbub of voices.

"Just a preaching service, I suppose," he answered.

"Let's go."

"You really want to?" He hesitated uncertainly.

"Yes. Let's go," she urged.

"All right. If you want to, we'll go," he consented without enthusiasm.

She interpreted his lack of enthusiasm as disinterest. But she was curious. If Mennonite Christmas customs were so old-fashioned and simple, what might their church services be like?

Lynette slipped into one of the rear

benches ahead of John. Only after they were seated did she realize the men and women sat on opposite sides of the building. She was the only woman on the men's side. She was embarrassed to have made such a blunder as soon as she arrived. "Should I go to the other side?" she whispered.

John shook his head. That would only cause more heads to turn. He knew other visiting couples had sat together before. Even though he knew better, they would be excused for Lynette's sake.

She was quiet and attentive throughout the service. There was nothing unusual about it as far as he could see. There was the normal amount of visiting afterward. Many people introduced themselves and said how nice it was to see them both there. Still, John was uncomfortable.

"That was really cute," Lynette giggled as they started back to the farm to spend the night. "All those white caps on one side and black suits on the other. I didn't know what was going on when they all turned around and got on the floor the first time. You didn't tell me that's how they pray. The singing was good though," she rattled on. "I never heard such good four-part singing from a congregation. Still, it's funny not to have any choir or organ. The church wasn't even decorated for

157

Christmas—no candles or flowers or anything. There weren't even any drapes at the windows!"

"You don't need to make fun," John's tone was clearly defensive. "We can worship without organs and choirs and fancy trimmings."

"We! Next you are going to tell me you want to be a Mennonite again," she bristled.

"I didn't say that," he retorted. "I just don't like you making fun of my people. They have their way of doing things. Just because it's different from your way, doesn't mean there's anything wrong with it."

"I didn't know you thought so much of 'your people,'" she mocked.

John drove the rest of the way in silence. He was sure the two of them would be talked about for days afterward. He could almost hear all the wagging tongues saying, "Did you see John and his wife? . . . Norman and Ida must feel terrible about it . . . I wonder why John turned out that way . . . Isn't it too bad he married a girl like that . . ." and on and on.

He could not understand his own feelings. He was not wishing to go back to his church, and he knew Lynette would never go with him if he did go back. But strangely, he felt personally insulted when she poked fun at his people; for in spite of everything, they were still his people, and he could not deny it. He did not know himself what he really thought about anything. He wished he had never gone to church. It was all too confusing. He did not want to think about it.

Chapter 17

Winter was wearing itself out, and John's patience with his wife was also wearing thin. He found it impossible to overlook her casual approach toward housekeeping any longer. He ached for the home cooking and spotless housekeeping of his childhood.

"Aren't you ever going to clean up this place?" he'd wail after stumbling over a pair of her shoes and kicking them out of the way.

"I'm working as many hours as you. Or have you forgotten?" She stifled a yawn.

"Why don't you quit and keep a decent house?"

"You don't seem to mind when payday comes. I was trained to be an RN, not a housekeeper."

"That's easy to see."

"Sit there, you oaf, and complain. You'd

never think of helping, would you?"

"I wasn't trained to be a housekeeper either. Mom could keep house without Pop's help."

"Rooty-toot-toot for her! She didn't work, either."

"I'd say she did. You don't know anything about housekeeping. I can't stand living in a rat nest. If you'd just put your things away as soon as you are done with them, it wouldn't get so cluttered."

"You are the most tactless . . . If you know so much about it, you can have the job. Help yourself. Your dear mother may have been a perfect housekeeper, but I'm not going to be a slave to any house."

After several variations of the argument, John finally decided he had three options. He could continue the fruitless sessions of arguing on the subject, learn to live with the clutter, or keep after it himself. He chose the latter. He was weary of the battle.

Keeping the house presentable was not too difficult. He had been used to keeping his own room neat. But cooking had always been a mystery to him. He was not interested in adding culinary skills to his housekeeping duties. Unfortunately, Lynette's knowledge of cooking was not much greater than his own. Not only did she not know how to cook very well, she was not excited about learning. Occasionally, a burst of industriousness overtook her, and she made an attempt. Then John would be hopeful things were taking a turn for the better. But her bursts of domesticity were as brief as they were intense.

Once, John was fortunate enough to wish aloud for his old favorite of pot pie at a time that coincided with one of these rare bursts of activity. Unfortunately, the pot pie he remembered was something with which she was not familiar. She offered him a dish of diced chicken, peas, and cubed potatoes under a biscuit topping. She expected him to exclaim delightedly over her pot pie and was disappointed when he made no comment, though he ate a generous serving.

When he began wiping his plate clean with a half slice of bread, as his father had always done, she jumped up and snatched his plate away.

"We use dessert plates, you know," she snapped. His habit was crude and vulgar to her, though she usually only made fun of it.

"What's eating you?" John looked up in surprise.

"Nothing," she said icily.

He knew better. "Yes, there is," he insisted.

"I spend hours making the pot pie you rave about, and then you sit there and shovel it in without so much as a word. I may as well make beans from a can."

"That wasn't pot pie!" He was puzzled.

"Oh, it wasn't?" she bristled. "Then what do *you* think pot pie is? The cookbook calls this pot pie."

"My mother never put peas in pot pie. And it wasn't baked like that. It had chicken and potatoes in it with some sort of square noodles. She made her own dough for the noodles," he tried to explain.

"Tell me more," she mocked. "I long to hear all about your blessed mother's cooking and housekeeping. She never measured anything when she cooked, did she?"

"Not usually," he admitted uneasily.

"She was a natural-born cook," Lynette rushed on. "She could milk cows, make the whole family's clothes, keep a big garden, and can hundreds of jars of food every year. With a flick of her wrist she could make homemade rolls, bread, doughnuts, apple pie, and pot pie like no one ever heard of."

"It's in the Mennonite cookbook, I'm sure. Becky and Ken gave us one for a wedding gift. If you look in there maybe you'll see what I mean," he tried to be helpful.

"Humph!" she snorted, thoroughly angry

163

now. "Mennonites are so special they even have their own cookbook. *I* am not a Mennonite. I don't intend to be—or cook like one. If all you wanted was a Mennonite cook, why didn't you marry one? Why did you marry me?"

John stared at his wife's flushed face. His eyes bored into hers. "Why did I marry you? You know why. What I'd like to know is — why did *you* marry *me*?"

"To win a bet," she blurted without thinking.

John stood up. He looked down on his wife. "What did you say?" he asked slowly and distinctly.

Her face blanched. In her anger she had revealed what she intended to keep a secret forever. "N-Nothing," she stammered, fear replacing anger.

"I thought you said you married me to win a bet." He was master now. "Is that correct?" There was no response. "Look at me," he demanded, putting a finger under her chin and tilting her face up toward his. "Is that what you said?"

She reached up and hugged him hard. She nodded and sniffed. "I'm sorry. You are sweet, and I am lucky to have you."

Her sudden change of heart de-escalated the battle. He sat down again and she slipped into his lap.

"Would you mind telling me who you won the bet against?" he asked presently.

"I wasn't going to tell you," she pouted prettily, knowing it was too late to escape now. "If you must know, it was Nancy Peters."

"How much?" he continued to pry.

"A hundred dollars." This with downcast eyes.

He looked at her incredulously, silently. "So that $100 was more than a wedding gift," he said at last. "What did you do with it?"

"I used it to get your recliner," she confessed.

So that was it! She had always firmly refused to tell where she had gotten the money for his expensive Christmas gift. Though he had always enjoyed relaxing in his chair, now suddenly he was repulsed by the sight of it. It was bought with blood money. Wordlessly, he pushed her off his lap and stood up. In slow motion, he turned and crossed the room.

"John! Where are you going?" she cried as he opened the door.

He cursed her rudely and banged the door behind him.

He walked the streets, not knowing and little caring where he went. He was sick at heart and disgusted with both himself and his wife. Where was the demure, reserved girl she had been when he first learned to know her? Either he had not known what she was really like or she had changed drastically. She had tricked him into marriage to win a bet. Did she love him at all? He remembered vividly the day at the lake and the passionate night that followed. He had been so sure he loved her and she loved him. Piecing things together now, he deduced that all her actions were coolly calculated moves toward winning her bet. *Of all the rotten deals!* He slammed his fist into a corner lamppost savagely. *Women! Dirty, scheming women! And I was naive enough to think she married me for love. I don't care if I never see her again!*

Alone in the apartment, Lynette cursed herself for the angry, thoughtless remark. She wished fervently it could be recalled. It was true she had won a bet when she married John, but that was not the only reason she had wanted him. The idea of marrying a Mennonite was sort of novel. She had found his parents' way of life quaint and amusing. She took an odd sort of satisfaction in the knowledge that he was willing to leave behind all his relatives and friends for her. Now, she feared their hold on him was stronger than she had imagined. He had not thrown away over twenty years of teaching and influence in a matter of months. His ideas of a good time, a home, even the handling of finances were terribly conservative and old-fashioned to her way of thinking. What he called good management, she called stinginess. She thought he was picky about details that to her were unimportant. His idea of a good time was a quiet evening at home while she longed to go places and do things. They seemed to be at opposite ends of the poles.

He might divorce me! she thought with alarm. She knew the state would give him legal grounds for a divorce because she coerced him into marriage through deception. But she did not want that to happen. She knew she had hurt him deeply. It would not easily be forgotten. She would try hard from now on to please him. He had loved her before and she was sure she could make him love her again.

Having vented his feelings on the lamppost, John felt the bottled anger and humiliation draining away and being replaced by an unutterable weariness. He rested his forehead on his arm and leaned against the post. How long he remained in this position, he did not know.

"Having trouble, son?" a sympathetic voice at his elbow asked. John looked up at the policeman and nodded vaguely. "Anything I can do?"

"No," he answered thickly. What could a policeman do about any of the mess he was in? There was nothing anyone could do. Even God Himself could not change what was done. No one could do anything.

"Sure you don't want a lift home?"

"No, thanks. I'll be all right," John said with an assurance he did not feel. Nothing would ever be all right again. With heavy feet, he turned and headed back to the apartment and Lynette. There was nowhere else to go.

She heard his key in the lock, flew to meet him and threw herself into his arms. "John! I'm so glad you came back," she breathed. "I was worried about you. It's so cold out there tonight. I'm sorry you were upset. Please say you'll forgive me. I truly do love you."

Her warmth and sweet smell melted some of his anger. He was not sure he could ever forget the humiliation of being the grand prize in a sweepstakes. But she was his wife, and she could be very sweet when she wanted to be.

"We won't ever talk about it again," he said, giving her shoulders a slight squeeze.

She kissed him with all the ardor she possessed and rubbed the back of his neck in acceptance of the half-forgiveness he had expressed.

"I am wicked," she said playfully, "and I know it. But you are so dear. I just had to have you at any cost. I would have married you, bet or no bet. That was just a bonus thrown in."

"I said—we won't talk about it again," he repeated grimly. "How about making me a cup of coffee?"

She hurried to fill the request. She knew she had said enough. It was time for actions now, not words.

Chapter 18

Several months of comparative peace followed Lynette's resolve to reform. She made a sincere effort to please John. He responded by being more helpful in the house and even the kitchen. She changed her mind about postponing a family for several years. A baby, she now felt, would be a unifying force in their marriage, which seemed to have gotten off to a poor start. John was delighted when she returned home from the doctor's office with the confirmation that they were indeed going to be parents. She was a little surprised and amused at the depth of his pleasure at this turn of events.

"I hope it's a boy," he grinned, giving her a playful swat.

"Oh, but little girls can be dressed so prettily," she differed.

"Every father wants a son," he said firmly. "If this one isn't a boy, we'll try again next year."

She rolled her eyes. "Mercy! Let's have this one first. You know," she changed the subject, "this apartment is too small for even one child. We'll have to hunt for a bigger place. I want a house, not an apartment. It should have a nice kitchen, a fireplace, at least three bedrooms, and two baths. I could decorate the one bedroom for a nursery . . ." she dreamed.

"It should have an acre of lawn," he joined in, "lots of trees for a boy to climb and build a tree house in, room for a dog . . ."

She laughed. "Let's look in the paper and see if there is anything like that."

Finding her dream house seemed to become an obsession with her. She dragged him from property to property in search of a house. He agreed they needed more room than the tiny, three-room apartment if they were going to have a family. But once again, their ideas of a house did not mesh. If he saw something he thought he could handle on his paycheck, she would not even consider it. Everything she liked was too expensive for him.

After they returned from another fruitless day of house hunting, Lynette sank into the recliner and sighed. "I don't know why you have to be so stubborn. Everything that is nice, you say is too expensive. We are going to have a mortgage no matter what we buy. We might as well get something nice while we're at it."

"But don't forget, when the baby comes we'll only have one paycheck. The payments on the places you like would be more than I could make on my pay alone," he pointed out.

"Then get a better-paying job," she said as if it were that simple. "Your two years at the hospital were up last month. You are free to go somewhere else."

"And what do you propose I should do?"

"What did you do before you came to Allendale? Surely you have some kind of training. You don't expect to mow lawns and paint walls all your life, do you?"

"I kind of like the maintenance work," he said thoughtfully. "As for training, I guess I was trained to work with my hands."

"Didn't you go to college?"

"College! My dear lady, I didn't even graduate from high school."

"You're a dropout?" She was shocked.

"I'm afraid so," he said. "That's not so terrible, is it? My parents thought learning to work on the farm was an education in

172

itself. I helped Pop on the farm until about a year before I went into IW. Then I worked with a carpenter crew."

"Didn't you ever want to do anything better? You could make much more money as a stock broker—or something." She searched frantically for ideas. "There is money in real estate or insurance."

"No thanks," he shook his head. "That doesn't appeal to me. What's wrong with making a living with my hands?"

"But that's so plebeian!" she cried. "You don't want to be a common laborer all your life."

"I don't want to, or you don't want me to?" he questioned. "As long as I earn an honest living, I don't mind being a common laborer."

"You're impossible!" She was exasperated. "Can't you see? If you had a *position*, not just a job, we could afford a better house."

"But I don't qualify for a position, so we'll just have to settle for what we can afford," he closed the argument.

Lynette knew she had lost this round and did not reply. She was a little more reasonable in her search for a house, but her choices were still more than he thought they could afford. Eventually, she found a house she simply had to have. John listened with growing alarm as she described it.

173

"It's the neatest place," she bubbled. "It's only a year old. It's a two story Colonial house on a big wooded lot in the Mockingbird Hill development. The house has four bedrooms and two and a half baths, a solid oak kitchen, and a dishwasher. There's a big bay window in the dining area, and there is a formal dining room besides. It has a family room with a fireplace and a wet bar. There is an office and laundry on the first floor. Out back there is a concrete patio and a sunroom with a quarry tile floor. It has the most beautiful spiral staircase going up the two full stories inside the foyer. The whole interior is finished in neutral shades, so any kind of decorating would be possible. It has an attached two-car garage, central air conditioning and electric heat. It's *everything* we want."

"And did you find out what the price tag is on this dream house?" he asked when he could finally get a word in edgewise.

"It is a little more than you thought you could pay, but when you see it, I know you'll just love it," she hedged.

"How much?"

"$53,000," in a meek voice. "But it's worth it," she hurried on.

"Is that all?" he mocked. "That's a lot more than we can afford and you know it."

"But John!" she pleaded. "You haven't seen it. It has trees for a boy to climb and build a tree house in, room for a dog . . . It has everything! At least come with me to see it. It doesn't cost anything to look."

"Oh, all right," he consented grudgingly. "But it's a waste of time. We can't afford it, and I'm not buying it."

Lynette would not let the matter rest. She pouted and begged, using every argument she could conceive in her favor.

"But honey," he tried to reason, after they had seen the house, "what do you think we'll use for money for the payments. You know you will soon quit working and we'll have to live on my paycheck. The mortgage payments are $200 a month."

"I can go back to work as soon as the baby is born," she offered.

"I told you before, I want my child to have a full-time mother. You are not going back to work. We'll live on what we can afford on my pay."

"You earn twice the amount of the payments in a month," she argued.

"You are forgetting we'll have to pay taxes and utilities, too. We would need to buy furniture since this apartment is furnished. And we'll have another mouth to feed soon."

"Babies don't eat much," she disagreed.

"You'll hardly notice the difference on the grocery bill."

"Maybe not at first, but there are other things besides food to provide. What will it cost to decorate your nursery and outfit it the way you want? Probably more than you think," he answered his own question.

"You old tight wad!" She cursed and there were sparks in her eyes. "I'm sure it would all work out somehow. You just don't want me to have a nice house. You don't love me."

"Yes, I do," he sighed. "I'm just trying to use good judgment. I've gone over it more than once trying to figure out a way to do it. If we had two paychecks coming, maybe we could swing it. But it's impossible on one."

"If only you would get another job and earn more!" she wailed.

"The only way I can earn more is by moonlighting," he said.

"Then moonlight."

"Are you serious?"

"Of course I'm serious," she cried. "I want that house!"

"I wouldn't be home much if I had two jobs," he pointed out.

"I'm not afraid to be alone."

"It means that much to you?"

"I'll never be happy if we don't get that house."

"All right." He took a deep breath. "If it's that important, I'll get a second job. I'll never have any peace unless you get what you want," he surrendered at last. He was weary of the battle that had gone on for weeks and saw she would keep after him until she got her way.

"John! You're wonderful!" she cried, throwing her arms around him. "Call them right away and tell them we'll take it. Quick, before somebody else gets it."

"I doubt if that would happen with the price they're asking," he remarked dryly. "I must be the world's biggest fool."

"You won't regret it," she promised. "We'll be completely happy there."

Much as he dreaded going so deeply into debt, it almost seemed to be worth it after all. Lynette lived in a feverish state of excitement and activity that fall after they bought and moved into the lovely house. She seemed more contented than ever before in their year of married life. She fairly purred as she selected the furniture, drapes and accessories for the rooms they would occupy. John was firm that the extra bedrooms remain empty until they needed them, and she consented on this point. She quit her job in order to have everything finished and perfect by the time the baby arrived. He was happy to see her happiness.

John found a second job pumping gas at a truckstop. He worked six hours each evening and all day Saturday. He knew the job embarrassed Lynette, but she said nothing, knowing it was her insistence on the house that was the cause. The pace was exhausting, though the work was not that strenuous. He saw Lynette only briefly over a hurried supper in his dash from job to job. She was always asleep when he came home after midnight and slept late in the mornings, pleading fatigue due to her condition. He helped himself to a bowl of cold cereal in the mornings and left quietly so as not to disturb her. She was usually bright and cheerful over supper, chattering eagerly about her latest purchases and redecorations.

With his full work schedule, John had no time to shop with his wife. She bought the newest and finest of everything. By the time the house was done to suit her, he needed to take out an additional loan to cover the bills she left in her wake like a trail of fallen leaves. If she had not been so cheerful and optimistic, he would not have allowed her to spend as she did. She even seemed to take more interest in housekeeping now that she had her coveted house. It was a high price to pay for her happiness, and he knew they would be strapped to their debt for years. But if she would at last become a happy wife and mother, it might be worth it.

Christmas that year was spent quietly at home awaiting the imminent birth of their child. The baby was born in early January. It was a boy, just as John had said it would be. Lynette chose the name of Todd Austin. John was not especially fond of the name. But he had not given much thought to the matter of a name and had nothing else to suggest. So Todd Austin Shenk was entered on the birth certificate.

John could barely wait the five days Lynette was in the hospital. He longed to hold his son, not just see him through the nursery window. When they finally had him at home, John thrilled at the nearly weight-less touch of the infant cradled in his arms. This was his son. He was a *father*. It was a wonderful feeling. Their home and joy were now complete. He envisioned years of work-ing, playing, and learning together as Todd grew from the innocence of this baby into boyhood, adolescence and maturity. The miracle of life lay asleep in his arms. He was overwhelmed with the wonder of it all. Surely the best part of life was just ahead and even now beginning.

Chapter 19

Todd was a fat, healthy baby. He cried only to make his needs known and required very little extra attention. Lynette's mother had come every day for a week to help with the running of the house. But the new parents soon insisted they were able to manage alone, and she left the little family to themselves.

Lynette was happy in her new role as mother. John deeply resented now the second job that had been forced upon him. The minutes he was able to spend with his son were few in number, and because of it, increased in value. His first awkwardness at holding the tiny bundle quickly passed. In his rush from job to job each evening, he rumpled and tossed his son until Lynette took Todd away, protesting he would injure the infant. John was pleased to see her motherliness, but chaffed inwardly at the same time. She had all day to play with Todd; he had only a few minutes. She could not understand the unfulfilled hungers of his brand new father's heart.

John's parents brought their family to see the new grandchild on the Sunday Todd was two weeks old. John's pride when he showed them his son was evident. Ida brought a meal in order to spare Lynette the trouble of cooking for guests. It was a common gesture and John never gave it a second thought. But Lynette could not help resenting it. Somehow she felt it was a slight against her abilities. John's two youngest brothers and the twins sat primly on chairs. They were clearly uncomfortable in the fine house and definitely visitors. Marlin, who had brought Jane with him, had come both to see the baby and to say good-by. He would be leaving the next week to begin two years of voluntary service in British Honduras.

John enjoyed the visit immensely and was sorry the time passed so quickly. It was good to visit with Mom and Pop, learn the news from home, and eat Mom's cooking again.

John's mother loved Todd on sight, as John had known she would. Todd looked so much like John when he had been a baby, she said. How swiftly the years had flown! Where and what would this child be twenty years from now? Would he have a proper Christian upbringing? He was innocent now, but so soon he would be learning and absorbing values as they were lived around him. Would John take the time to teach him? Would Lynette be a real mother? Only time could tell. Ida's thoughts and fears could not be expressed. Though Lynette was her daughter-in-law and politely courteous, they could not share as a mother and daughter would, for they did not think alike in too many areas. They were merely two acquaintances brought together as relatives through circumstances, not deliberate choice.

When the visit ended, John's parents returned home cautiously optimistic. Though their son was not what they would have chosen him to be, he seemed to be doing well. They had a nice house, and Lynette seemed to be a good mother. Perhaps things would be all right after all. So far as they could tell, things were going smoothly and John was happy. They had no way of knowing how wide the differences were that were beginning to grow between their son and his wife. The smooth surface was frothing underneath. The latest in their series of differences had arisen soon after the birth of

Todd when Lynette began making plans for his baptismal service.

"Baptize him?" John was aghast. The thought of baptizing his son had never entered his mind.

"Of course!" She did not understand his reaction. "Why not?"

"He's just a baby," he said as if that explained everything.

"Of course," she said again. "That's why he should be baptized."

"*My* son isn't going to be baptized while he's a baby," John said firmly.

"But he must be." She was bewildered at his refusal. "Do you want him to be a heathen?"

"He won't be a heathen if he isn't baptized," John argued. "Baptism at his age means nothing. He isn't old enough to know what he is doing."

"That's what *you* think. I was baptized when I was a baby. Todd is my child too, in case you have forgotten. And I want him baptized," she insisted stubbornly.

Ignoring John's protests, she proceeded with the arrangements for the baptism, which would be held when Todd was two months old. She reluctantly agreed not to invite John's parents. It would be irregular not to have both sets of grandparents there to witness the baptism. But he knew his parents' beliefs on infant baptism. He wanted to spare them the awkward position of participating in something that was entirely opposed to their beliefs, and of which he was not in favor himself. Lynette decided she could easily manufacture some excuse for their absence because of the distance that separated them.

"I can't see why you think this has to be," John protested as they dressed for Todd's baptism. "You never go to church any other time. What happened to you anyway? You used to go to church before we were married. We have hardly been there since. You always had some excuse. I thought you were a Christian when I married you."

"Of course I'm a Christian!" she exclaimed. "You don't think I'm a heathen, do you?"

"No," he said lamely. "I'm just trying to figure out why you used to go to church and now you don't anymore."

"That's easy. I went because I thought you were a religious person—being in IW and all," she said shortly. "I didn't know you cared. You never mention it. Go to church if you want to. I don't care."

"I don't want to go alone," he countered. "But we should go for Todd's sake. He should go to Sunday school."

"He's too little for that yet. We'll send him when he's old enough," she waved the matter aside. "As far as I'm concerned, we need the church for baptisms, weddings, and funerals. Other than that, Christmas and Easter are enough for me. I don't need to go every week."

John sat tensely through the Sunday morning service. He dreaded the ordeal of the baptism and wished he could escape it somehow. He remembered his own baptism as a teen-ager. He could not recall exactly what he had promised, but he knew he had broken his vows repeatedly. His conscience smote him as he looked at the blissfully innocent child Lynette held. If he, as an adult, had not kept his baptismal vows, how could this child have any chance of doing so? Would his son grow up to be a disappointment to him as he knew he had been to his father? For the first time, he became painfully aware of the huge responsibility of being a father. The son he had helped to create was also his to mold and teach. He felt woefully inadequate to teach another when he was not doing what he knew was right himself.

His reverie was broken when he heard the pastor say, "As you have noticed in your bulletin, Mr. and Mrs. John Shenk have requested baptism for their son. Will you please come forward?"

John and Lynette rose and walked together to the front of the sanctuary where the pastor waited.

"Christianity is more caught than taught," the pastor began. "The role of the parents is the most important factor in a child's life in teaching him to become a follower of Christ. It is not water, but faith in Christ that saves. Only God knows those who are truly His. As parents of this child, I will therefore ask you: Is it your desire that this child become a follower of Christ? Will you commit yourself to the task of presenting the Gospel of Christ to him?"

"Yes," both parents answered together.

"Name this child," the pastor said.

"Todd Austin," John answered according to Lynette's previous coaching.

The pastor took Todd and carried him to a basin of water mounted on a marble pedestal. He dipped his finger into the water three times, making a cross on Todd's forehead each time as he said, "I baptize you, Todd Austin, in the name of the Father, and of the Son, and of the Holy Ghost. Amen."

Todd blinked and looked at the pastor solemnly. It almost seemed as if he understood the words he was hearing.

"Shall we pray," the pastor intoned.

There was a soft rustle and then silence except for the voice of the pastor rising and falling as he dedicated Todd to God. As the pastor prayed, John's uneasiness slowly vanished. The things the pastor was saying sounded a lot like what he had been taught to believe. It was only the age of the one being baptized that was vastly different. Perhaps no harm had been done in going along with this ceremony. If it satisfied Lynette, he was satisfied. He followed the prayer, dedicating himself to the task of rearing Todd for God. His heart echoed the solemn "Amen" as the prayer ended.

The pastor turned to face the congregation and lifted Todd high in the air for them to see as he challenged them to be faithful to God and the church for the sake of the child he was presenting to them. "Will you support this child in the work God calls him to do in the life of the church?" he asked.

The congregation murmured their assent. The pastor turned again and gave the wondering child to his mother. "God bless you all," he said simply in a low tone. "You may return to your seats."

Lynette beamed with pride as the little family returned to their pew. She was proud of her son's magnificent behaviour during the ceremony and John's cooperation even though she knew he had consented grudgingly. Todd had performed very well. He would be a model child and someday a handsome, intelligent, successful man who would make her the envy of all the other mothers she knew. She would insist on the best of everything for him. He would have an education that would open doors which remained closed to his father. He would be her life-long source of pride and joy.

Chapter 20

Lynette sighed and pulled herself out of bed when Todd's wails became insistent. She had not bothered to get up when John left for work. She had been up with Todd several times during the night and did not feel like getting up until she had to. The day stretched long and monotonously ahead. It would be another treadmill of bottles, diapers, meals, and laundry.

The newness of motherhood lost its glory as it became routine. Preparing formula, washing diapers, feeding, bathing, and all the physical needs of caring for Todd were not hard work. He was a contented baby. But time hung heavily on her hands with John working both jobs. Their social life was nonexistent. She began to have second thoughts about the situation. She longed to go out for an evening, but it was impossible. When John had off, he was too tired to go anywhere. She could hardly go out to dine and dance alone. She could see now what John had seen before they bought the house. But she would rather die than admit she had made a mistake.

Mournfully, she went through the motions of caring for Todd. She found no sense of fulfillment in the actions. She was tired of being cooped up in the house with only a baby for company. She longed to be one of the liberated women who were part of the work force and not the family servant. But John would not hear of her returning to work. Every time she suggested it, he firmly refused. It was his job to earn the living and hers to keep the house and care for Todd, he insisted.

Still nursing her grudge, she turned to the dreaded task of dishwashing. A forlorn-looking dish of garbage sat in the sink. John had forgotten to empty it when he went to work. In annoyance, she grabbed the dish and stalked to the garbage can outside the back door. *The thoughtless man!*

In a swift motion, she emptied the contents of the dish and slammed the lid back on the punget can. The warm spring sunshine smiled down benevolently and the moist smells of spring assaulted her nostrils. She sniffed appreciatively. Her irritation began to fade. It was such a lovely morning. The clear sky promised the day would continue in the same fashion. The winter had seemed endless and spring had come so demurely it was simply a weakened version of winter. But this early May morning it seemed as though spring had come in a rush. It was impossible to remain depressed on such a glorious morning.

Lynette felt her spirits rising with the temperature as she returned to the kitchen with the empty dish. It was warm enough for Todd to go outside. She would take him for a long walk. She had to get out of the house or go mad. In a burst of eagerness, she put on the baby's cap and sweater and set out on their small excursion as grandly as if they were going on a trip around the world.

She ambled slowly along, not especially caring where she went, and soaking up the sunshine like a wilted houseplant that has suddenly been transplanted. She was headed in the general direction of the business section of town and soon found herself among the stores. She stopped to admire an attractive display of summer clothes in a show window. Todd was getting heavy. She shifted him to her other arm and set the unavoidable diaper bag on the sidewalk.

"Lynette! What a surprise to see you!"

Lynette turned quickly. Her face lit up with pleasure. "Pamala! I haven't seen you since high school. What are you doing with yourself?"

"I'm a legal secretary for Schulze, Brown, and Leisawitz in Martinsburg. I'm in town to pick up some documents. And is this your baby?"

Lynette turned Todd to face her old friend. "Yes. This is Todd," she said proudly. "He's four months old."

"Oh, he's adorable!" Pamala cooed. "I didn't know you were married."

"Yes," Lynette repeated. "John and I were married about a year and a half ago. Are you married?"

"Not yet," Pamala laughed and flashed her ring finger to show her diamond. "But it won't be long. I'll be a June bride. I'm marrying James Brown—the Brown part of Schulze, Brown, and Leisawitz. Look! We have a lot of catching up to do. It's my lunch hour. Can you join me for lunch? My treat," she added as an afterthought.

"I'd love to," Lynette consented happily.

Lunch with Pamala was a refreshing change. The time passed much too quickly as the two old friends renewed their acquaintance and shared news of other mutual friends of their high school days. Lynette was grateful Pamala had offered to pay for the meal. She would have been mortified to admit she had no money. She satisfied Pamala's curiosity about John by explaining she had met her husband when he came to check on a patient in the ICU where she worked. Describing him as a technician gave Pamala no hint his technical tools were of the hardware store variety.

"I have to run," Pamala apologized, standing up. "I certainly enjoyed talking with you again."

"It's been nice seeing you, too," Lynette returned, picking up Todd and shouldering the diaper bag. "I should be getting Todd home anyway. He'll probably fall asleep before I get there. It's a long walk to Mockingbird Hill."

"You need a stroller," Pamala said.

"I know," Lynette agreed. "This is the first time it has been warm enough for Todd to be out. I didn't realize such a little fellow could get so heavy when I started out."

"Buy one before you start back," Pamala said as if it were as simple as that. "You'll probably be using it a lot from now on."

"That's true," Lynette agreed. "If I had the checkbook I believe I'd take your advice." She would never admit the checkbook balance was nearly zero.

"You don't need cash," Pamala said. "Put it on your credit card."

"I don't have that, either." Lynette grimaced. That was true enough. She and John had no credit cards.

"You are out of luck then," Pamala sympathized. "Better come more prepared the next time you decide to go for a walk."

"Oh, I'm tough," Lynette laughed as if she did not mind. "Don't worry. We'll take our time and have a lovely spring stroll."

The two friends parted ways, agreeing to meet again soon. Lynette went on her way, retracing her late morning steps. She felt somehow cheated. The smartly dressed, sophisticated Pamala made her feel like a dowdy matron in comparison. She was a poor housewife going back to her prison, while Pamala was an executive legal secretary going back to the important business world. Regardless of the impressions she had given her friend, she knew the truth. John was only a laborer and always would be. They would never fit into Pamala's world. She would always have to do without things Pamala took for granted.

Self-pity welled up again inside Lynette as she ambled along with her burdens. She stopped in front of a large department store to shift Todd again to her other arm. He had fallen asleep and was getting heavier and heavier. A sign on the front door arrested her attention. It offered a free gift to anyone who opened a charge account with their establishment. Pamala's suggestion had planted the seed of the idea in Lynette's mind. Now it mushroomed and propelled her into action.

Why not?, she reasoned. *Pamala's right. I'm going to need a stroller a lot from now on. If I open a charge account today, I can push Todd the rest of the way home and get a gift besides. I wonder if I can open an account without John?*

It was much more simple to open a charge account than she had imagined. Being his wife, she could utilize John's credit to open the account without obtaining his consent or approval. The account was opened in her name and the stroller purchased without any difficulty.

She left the store, happy once again, with Todd comfortably sleeping in the stroller. Her gift for opening the account and the diaper bag were safely stowed in the wire basket under the seat, leaving her hands free to push the stroller. She enjoyed the lei-surely walk home in style. It was surprising how fast the day had passed. It was the most interesting day that had come her way for a long time.

When she arrived home, Lynette laid Todd in the crib and put the stroller out of sight. She did feel a little guilty now about opening the charge account without John's knowledge. She knew he would object even though she was sure the low monthly payments could never be a hardship on the budget. By the time the first bill came and he learned of the account, she was sure she would think of a way to handle him.

The stroller was put to use many times as spring gave way to summer. Lynette was never sorry she bought it. As Todd grew bigger and heavier, it would have been impossible for her to carry him into town on their long walks. She proudly showed off her son to friends and strangers. He was a cheerful little soul who seemed to have an inborn talent for winning hearts. Building upon this personality trait, she dreamed of the important person he would become, for she was determined to "make something" of him. It gave her a sense of satisfaction to be among people, even though she was not a part of the business world.

She found it as easy to open a second charge account as it had been to open the first one. Soon her wallet grew fertile with the plastic money. It was so easy to get credit and buy on it.

Though Lynette was with Todd constantly, he seemed to have a special attachment to his father. It was for John that he first laughed aloud. He was a bright child, learning motor skills at an early age. John praised each new accomplishment lavishly. He was delighted to see Todd's mind develop. Lynette was absurdly jealous when Todd said "Da-da." After all the time she spent with him, she thought he should say "mama' first.

The joy of motherhood faded with the reality. Todd was well cared for physically, but Lynette increasingly regarded him as a burden. His coming had changed her life, interrupted her career, and destroyed her girlish figure. She had never enjoyed housework and now was trapped in it. Her depression and moodiness were reflected in Todd's behavior and her treatment of John. She consoled herself with shopping sprees until the mounting bills threatened to destroy them.

"You have *got* to stop spending," John insisted in despair as he tried to stretch the money to cover all the bills. "If we go any deeper into debt, we will lose the house. I just can't keep up with all the bills, even with two jobs."

"I can go back to work," Lynette offered. She knew he did not want that, but she kept hoping someday he would agree.

"I have a better idea. Give me all your credit cards," he suggested. "How many of them do you have anyway?"

"If you let me go back to work, I'll give you my credit cards," she bargained, ignoring his question.

"It's a deal!" He accepted her bargain so quickly she was stunned. "I didn't want you to go back to work, but we are up against it. We have to do something. If we both work full time, we will have more money than I can make with one full- and one part-time job. If you can get on the three-to-eleven shift at the hospital, we would need a babysitter for only a few hours a day. I could be with Todd evenings and you could still get some sleep before he wakes up in the morning." It was clear he had thought the matter out carefully beforehand.

Lynette kept her part of the bargain and reluctantly parted with her credit cards. She regretted now her quick proposition. She had felt safe in making it, for she had been sure he would not accept the offer. Yet, she was happy to be back at work again and feel like a useful person. She was pleased with the babysitter they found. Judy was a young mother with two children of her own. Her desire to babysit sprang as much from a heart of love for children as it did from the need of a little additional income. Both John and Lynette felt Todd was in good hands the two hours their shifts overlapped.

John was a little less than overjoyed to have a working wife. It made him feel somehow inadequate as head of the home. But it was the only way out that he could see. It gave the budget a lift and was a relief for his strained strength. The two jobs had him nearly exhausted. He reasoned that since Lynette had plunged them so deeply into debt, she could help to pay it off. At least if she was working she was not spending and adding to the debt. Most importantly, this new arrangement gave him many more hours to spend with Todd. The luxury of the extra time with his son made up for the less-than-ideal situation of a working wife. Everyone would be happier this way, he was sure.

Chapter 21

With John and Lynette working different shifts, some changes needed to be made in their schedules and duties. Lynette slept as long as Todd was quiet in the mornings. She seemed to accomplish very little in the housekeeping department before it was time to take Todd to the babysitter and go to work. The clutter of everyday living was not cleared away. The house lost its shine and looked shabby to John in spite of its expensive furnishings. From his earlier experience, he soon realized the housework would be his if he wanted it done. He kept after the clutter, but the place lacked a woman's touch. He added some cooking and, occasionally, laundry to his list of duties in addition to babysitting Todd. He had simply exchanged his paying job for housekeeping and had sent his wife to earn the second paycheck. In a way, he did not mind doing the housework, although he could never figure out what Lynette did during the hours she was home.

It was a joy to be with Todd. The child was pleasant and affectionate. The evenings with his son were John's favorite part of the day. He prepared simple but balanced meals and enjoyed feeding Todd. As he grew older, the baby foods and bottle were gradually replaced with finger foods and a training cup. John carried the baby with him wherever he went, in or out of the house, as he went about the housework. After Todd learned to walk, he was his father's faithful shadow. The two were inseparable.

Occasionally John waited up for Lynette to come home from work, but more often than not he was asleep when she came home. She did not waken him. In the mornings the procedure was reversed. He got up and went to work quietly without waking her. They communicated mainly by notes and mostly about chores around the house. Though husband and wife sharing a house, they seemed to revolve in separate circles. They were becoming strangers to each others' lives.

John was not pleased with this arrangement, but did not know what else to do. He had tried working two jobs himself and knew that was not the answer. He looked forward to the time when some of the debt would be paid and his wife could be at home again. It was only a temporary inconvenience, he consoled himself.

The excitement of going back to work soon dulled. As glad as Lynette was to get out of the house, the daily routine soon became monotonous and did not satisfy after all. She missed talking to John and the closeness they first had known. Less and less did she know what he was doing and thinking. Little things she would have told him were forgotten by the time she saw him awake and could tell him. Their physical relationship was minimal because of their conflicting schedules. She remembered their honeymoon and how pleasant everything had been then compared to the life they were now living. She was tired of never having enough money, tired of the endless treadmill of life. They never did anything but work, eat, and sleep, only to repeat the cycle day after day. The house she had thought would bring her so much happiness now had her working like a slave to support it. If they could get away from it all for awhile, perhaps they could recapture the magic of their honeymoon days and begin over.

Christmas was coming again. Their celebration would be on a limited scale this year, they both knew. For himself, John would not miss the lavish decorating and entertaining his wife thought was necessary. All he wanted was to be at home with his wife and son. He dreamed of sleeping in, having a lazy, cozy day with Todd and enjoying his antics together. They would choose a nice gift for him and simple ones for each other. He wished for nothing more. His greatest problem was deciding what to give Lynette. Their communication was so scanty he had no idea what she might need. He thought he might as well give her something practical that she needed around the house. Not arriving at any conclusions, he finally decided to ask her what she wanted.

"What could I get you for Christmas?" he asked on a Sunday morning when they were both home.

Lynette looked at her reflection in the mirror. Her hair had been cut in a short, easy-to-care-for style and her face looked bare without its make-up. *I'm getting old too young,* she thought regretfully. She was sure she saw lines beginning to form on her face. Suddenly she knew what she wanted. She wanted it desperately, more than any-

203

thing else.

"Oh, John!" she turned to face him, her eyes shining. "Let's go on a second honeymoon!"

"Second honeymoon?" he echoed.

"Yes!" She was excited. "Just the two of us."

"Where?"

She had not given the idea enough thought to have chosen a place. "Acapulco," she blurted out the first place that crossed her mind.

"Acapulco?!" He was incredulous.

"Why not?" she replied gaily. "It would be so nice and warm in Mexico this time of year. We might even win a fortune in the casinos."

"We can't afford it and you know it." His tone was flat. "Besides, we can't leave Todd."

"The cost be hanged," she retorted. "We can go now and pay later."

"We are already up to our ears in debt," he argued. "We can't afford one more thing on credit. Come on. Be more practical. Surely there is something you need around the house."

"What I need is to get away from it," she snapped shortly.

The subject was dropped and never reopened. After a lot of careful thought, he

204

finally chose a frilly peignoir set in the shade of blue that matched her eyes and a bottle of her favorite fragrance. He felt it was a compromise and hoped she would be satisfied. Surely she had not been serious about Acapulco. She had to know it was out of the question.

A few days before Christmas the nurses on Lynette's floor had a party. She expected John to accompany her as the other nurses' husbands did. But when the evening of the party arrived, John flatly refused to go. Todd was cutting teeth and had been running a slight fever all day.

"The sitter can take care of him as well as you," Lynette argued. "You don't have to stay with him."

"I don't have to, but I want to," he said, hoping she would decide to stay home too. "My son is more important to me than any old cocktail party. I'm not leaving him when he's sick to stand around all evening listening to a lot of empty talk that doesn't amount to a thing."

Her temper flared. "Are you implying I'm not a good mother if I go to this party?"

"Not at all," he said coolly. She knew he meant the exact opposite.

"Stay home with the kid and rot if you want to. You never go anywhere. If you won't go with me, I'll go alone," she threatened.

"Go," he said calmly, thinking she would not.

"I will," she announced, tossing her head. "And I'll have a good time, too," she threw over her shoulder as she went to get ready.

John sat in front of the TV with Todd on his lap. He had thought she would stay home if he refused to go. But having told her to go alone and seeing she intended to, he made no move to stop her or change his own mind about going. Silently, he sat, patting Todd's small bottom to comfort him and listening to the sounds of Lynette preparing to leave.

When she came down, her face carefully made up and dressed in her finest, he looked up. She stopped and looked at him, her eyes defying him to stop her. He turned back to the TV without speaking. She put her coat on and went out without a word. He heard the car back out of the drive and leave. He looked down at the moist little forehead of his son, shrugged, and suddenly did not care that she had gone. The times they were home together were rarely pleasant. Every little thing seemed to cause an argument. If they did their talking in notes, there were fewer disagreements. Todd was better company anyway.

Lynette did not truly enjoy the party, though she would not have admitted it. She felt rejected somehow by John's refusal to accompany her. His absence was awkward for her, but she invented an excuse she felt justified him.

Todd was not seriously ill, but the pain of cutting teeth made him unusually disagreeable. He was happy only if his father held and played with him. The moment John set him on the floor, he howled in protest. So they spent the evening playing patty-cake, going for piggyback rides, or anything else John could think of to amuse the child. He gave the chubby little fellow some baby aspirin and a cool sponge bath for his fever, keeping up a stream of small talk as he worked. Only one side of the conversation would have been intelligible to an audience, but the two understood each other perfectly. At length, Todd was dressed in clean pajamas and given a piggyback ride to bed. He lay down in the crib, immediately turned on his stomach and tucked his hands under him, signaling he was ready to sleep.

John pulled the blanket over him and patted him softly. "Nighty-night," he said, waving his hand.

Todd smiled weakly at his father, pulled one hand out from under him and returned the wave with a feeble flop of his hand.

"You dear little thing," John chuckled. He was thrilled at this new accomplishment. "You are precious. Go to sleep now and wake up feeling better." He turned off the light and left the room, leaving the door ajar so he would hear if Todd woke up and cried.

Even though it was early, John decided to go to bed too. The party would doubtless last at least until midnight. It was no use waiting up for Lynette, as sour as she had been when she left. But sleep eluded him. His thoughts turned to home, as they do the world over at Christmastime. They were not going to his family's Christmas dinner this year, much as he hated to miss it. They would visit his family another time, Lynette had promised. He did not have much faith in that promise, sincere as she made it sound. She always had an excuse if he mentioned making the trip. They had not been home for many months. Todd had grown so much since his family had last seen him. He wished they could see Todd now. He had reluctantly called home and told Pop they could not make the family dinner. Both John and Pop sensed the other's disappointment. The Shenks had all been looking forward to seeing Todd as much as John had been wanting to show him off.

Mentally, he compared the Christmas

they would have with the ones he had known at home. His life had turned out to be so different from what he had imagined five years ago. Without knowing why he should think of her, he remembered Miriam. He had heard she married a fellow she met at Bible School. She was living in one of the Midwestern states. He wondered what life might be like if he had married her as he once thought he would. Not that he wished now he had; he just wondered.

That shows how much anybody knows about the future, he thought. *Who would have guessed way back at Becky and Ken's wedding that Miriam would live in another state and that I would be where I am?*

Sleep came so softly he was not aware of falling asleep. He heard Lynette coming in hours later. She stumbled and swore roughly. Her unsteady steps approached the bedroom. He lay motionless, feigning sleep. She passed on to the bathroom and eventually returned to the bedroom. She slid into bed beside him and reached out to brush his face with her lips.

"You sleeping?" she murmured beguilingly.

Carefully, he controlled his slow breathing and did not answer. Her breath was stale and testified all too well of the "good time" she had been having.

Getting no answer, she turned her back to him and quickly fell asleep. She began snoring and he suddenly loathed her. Was this what he was working, scrimping, and slaving for? For this stinking, snoring, tipsy woman? She was not his idea of a loving wife. The gentle modesty and beauty which had attracted him to her were ashes. He felt hopelessly cheated and trapped by life.

I sure got myself into a mess, he thought morosely. *If somebody had told me when I went into IW that I'd be where I am today, I never would have believed it. I chose to go into IW instead of VS because I wanted to keep my car. If I had it to do over, I'd sell my car and go into VS like Marlin did.*

Marlin's letters were full of accounts of difficult, but rewarding experiences as he served in British Honduras. The small monthly allowance he received barely covered the cost of his personal needs. But he was richly rewarded in other ways too priceless to compute.

"Somehow, being down here, I've come to see life in a new perspective," he wrote. "At home we are so used to the life we live that we don't realize how the rest of the world lives. There is so much to be done, and so few are doing it. When I come home I want

210

to share my vision with other young people and open their eyes to the needs of the world. The harvest is ready, but the laborers are few."

John sighed deeply and tossed restlessly. Though Lynette was not the kind of wife he had expected her to be, he did not totally regret his marriage. From the union had come Todd, the one good thing that had happened to him in Allendale. The love of his son bound him to his situation with an indestructible tie. It was too late to change the course his life had taken. There was no point in fantasizing about what might have been if he had done differently.

Chapter 22

Lynette's spike heels clicked a rapid staccato as she came down the spiral staircase and crossed the tiles of the foyer. She stopped with her hand on the knob of the front door when John appeared in the doorway of the family room.

"Where are you going?" he asked mildly.

"Out," she said shortly.

"To the mailbox, I suppose?" he smirked.

"Pamala and I are going to an opera, if you must know," she said haughtily.

"Pamala," he said pensively. "Pamala again. You're with Pamala a lot these days, aren't you?"

"We're old friends." She was on the defensive.

"Seems that way," he assented. "Doesn't Pamala's husband like operas either?"

She shrugged. "He goes sometimes. They have season tickets. But something came up at the last minute and he couldn't go. Pamala didn't want to go alone so she offered me his ticket. *You* didn't want to go, did you?"

"To an opera? Are you kidding?" He laughed shortly. "I prefer Todd's company."

"I know."

The abrupt reply, poignant with meaning, hung between them as if suspended in the air. Turning, he went back into the family room.

"Have a good time." His words threw her insult back like a boomerang.

He bent and retrieved the evening paper from the floor. Sinking back into his chair, he stared unseeingly at the pages of newsprint. Somehow he could not quite believe her story, even though it appeared genuine. Lynette and Pamala went out together more often than he found credible. It did not seem natural for a newlywed couple to spend so much time apart as Pamala and her husband seemed to do. His and Lynette's work schedules provided them with so little mutual free time it was a rarity if they were home together. But lately it seemed she was never home. She had developed a circle of friends and a social life that did not interest him.

Even more disturbing than her absence

213

was her attitude toward him. She treated him with a cool detachment that puzzled him. She did not encourage or even seem to miss the little attention she had once expected of him. It seemed she needed him only to pay the bills. Looking back over the last year, it was easy to see their marriage had deteriorated badly. Their third anniversary had passed unnoticed. It was strange she had made no mention of it. Much as he tried, he could not put his finger on anything that was causing the decline. Nor did he know what to do to try to change things. The thing that puzzled him most was her improvement in keeping the house neat and tidy. He was glad to see her taking more interest in housekeeping, but he could not understand what had caused the change.

Todd interrupted John's reverie by pushing a tractor and wagon under his father's newspaper. "Fix it, Daddy," he begged.

John laid both the paper and his melancholy thoughts aside. He hooked the tractor and wagon together and set them on the floor. Then he dropped to his knees beside Todd, joining in his play. Subconsciously, John compensated for the lack of marital love by lavishing more love on Todd. The growing child absorbed and thrived on his father's love, responding in his own simple ways.

Lynette had once been extremely jealous of Todd's preference for John, but now she seemed not to mind. Todd was rapidly changing from a baby into a little boy. He was a curious toddler who was learning to talk. He knew many words and spoke simple sentences. John was delighted to see the child's mind develop and loved teaching him new things.

The evening passed in companionable harmony. Only the absence of a wife and mother marred its perfection. But father and son had grown so accustomed to the gap in the family circle it did not seem strange to them. There was no point in waiting up for her to return. John put Todd to bed at the usual time and took a leisurely shower before going to his own bed.

Slipping between the sheets, he lay on his back staring at the ceiling. His suspicions forced themselves to the forefront again as the silence and darkness enveloped him.

Is Lynette with Pamala tonight like she said or is she with someone else? Is that why she doesn't need me anymore? Is she running around with another man behind my back? But she couldn't. She just couldn't do that to me! I'd die if that happened!

The very thought made him sick to his stomach. A surge of loneliness engulfed him as he lay staring into the darkness. Somehow he felt detached from himself. The carefree youth he had once been was an altogether different person from the man he was now.

What's wrong with me? I feel like a useless heel. I know Lynette is ashamed of me. Why didn't she marry somebody else if she wanted a rich, important husband? Todd is the only one who needs me anymore. If it weren't for him, I'd feel like a total failure.

His suspicions aroused, John watched Lynette's actions more closely than ever before. Though he said nothing, he was constantly alert for clues that would prove she was having a secret affair. Yet, the idea his wife would actually be unfaithful to him was too foreign to his concept of marriage to seem a real possibility. He simply could not believe she would do a thing like that to him. But as he watched and observed, the evidence slowly mounted.

She wore new clothes and jewelry he had not bought, nor was he billed for them. He found a pack of cigarettes lying on the mantle that was not the brand he smoked. The bar was always well stocked though empty bottles were frequently in the garbage can. He knew he was not replenishing the supply and neither was his wife. He knew how much she earned and what her paycheck was used for.

He did not know where she got the money to buy all these things. Just when he had finally explained away to himself the reason for one discovery, another presented itself. He vacillated between belief and doubt.

When Todd's second birthday came, John wished they could have a little family party. But he and Lynette both had to work and it was impossible to get the three of them together at a suitable time. The decorated cake Lynette had bought was already cut and partly eaten when John and Todd had supper. But he lit the candles and sang "Happy Birthday" for Todd anyway. He knew birthdays are so exciting for a two-year-old that Todd would not object to the used candles and incomplete cake.

When they finished their private party of two, John washed Todd's hands and face, set him on the floor and began clearing the table. Todd ran to his toy chest and quickly came back.

"See, Daddy," he said, holding up a blue plush puppy. "Tom comed."

Tom? What is he talking about? "Did Mommie give you a pretty puppy?" he asked, looking at the toy.

Todd shook his head. "No. Tom comed," he repeated. "Tom say, 'gr-r-r-r,'" he laughed.

John looked at Todd strangely. *Tom? The T on the man's handkerchief I found. It fits together. Lynette is having an affair with some Tom right under my own roof. I'll find out what's going on around here before I'm a day older,* he thought angrily. *This has gone on long enough. Knowing the truth can't be any worse than not knowing for sure. I'll wait until she comes home from work and make her tell me. No. I won't. I'll do one better. I'll catch them in the act. Then she can't lie to me. Two can play this game.*

Craftily, John made his plans to trap Lynette and her lover. It would not do to let her suspect he had learned the truth. He wondered how many people knew what was going on. Who could tell him the most likely time to catch them? *But how can I ask anyone such a question? No. I'll just have to take a chance on it,* he thought grimly.

His heart hammered and his hands were clammy when he stealthily approached his house the next forenoon. He had parked a distance away and walked silently toward the house, screening his approach as much as possible.

How do I know which room they are in? If they see me coming, the guy might get away. I hope I can look innocent if he's not here.

Noiselessly, he entered the small door in

the garage. A white Cadillac was parked inside. *He's here! The scoundrel!*, John thought with both triumph and dismay. The hood of the car was still slightly warm. *He must have arrived recently.*

The house was quiet. John padded across the carpeted floors, careful not to trip or make any noise. Now he knew why Lynette kept the house presentable. She was not doing it for him, but to impress her lover.

Silently, he tiptoed around the corner to the family room. Softly, he opened the door. His face blanched at the repulsive sight that met his eyes. He stood speechlessly rooted to the spot. Lynette stood close to a man at the bar, her eyes fixed adoringly on him as he filled two cocktail glasses. He was an older man, carefully coiffured and graying at the temples. His hands looked as if they had never seen a day of manual labor.

Uncannily sensing they were being watched, Lynette turned. Expressions of surprise and defiance swiftly chased each other across her face. The words the man had been speaking broke off in mid-sentence as his gaze followed Lynette's to John.

John looked at him long and meaningfully. He wanted to beat the guy to a pulp, but he was momentarily paralyzed. The man looked so guilty, John was suddenly struck with the irony of the situation. He laughed contemptuously and without a word, motioned toward the door. Like a whipped dog, slinking away with its tail between its legs, the man slipped out the door.

Lynette knew the end had come. She was surprised, in a way, that she had been able to conceal her affair this long. Her incredible excitement had been mixed with guilt. It was almost a relief to face the issue.

Anger exploded like a tidal wave in John's brain. "Of all the dirty, low-down tricks!" His voice rose to a crescendo and cracked. "Just how long has this been going on?"

"For a couple of months," she confessed, tilting her chin defiantly. "And it's all your own fault."

"*My* fault?" He was stunned.

"Yes, your fault," she repeated. "All you ever want to do is sit at home and go to work. You never did anything for me."

"On the contrary," he objected. "Everything I did was for you."

"Really?" Her voice was silky-smooth and loaded with sarcasm. "I never would have guessed it. It's always Todd this and Todd that. He's always more important to you than I am."

"And how do you think *I* feel?" he shot back. "While I'm out working to pay your bills, you are entertaining another man in my house behind my back."

"So?" She tossed her head.

"You promised to love, honor, and cherish as long as we both live. Doesn't that mean anything to you?"

"If you think I'm going to spend all my life in this kind of dead-end living, you're crazy. All you wanted me for was to wash your clothes, cook your meals, and have your babies. You wanted me to be a baby factory like your wonderful mother. You were talking about a second baby before we ever had the first one. I don't want that kind of life. I want to have some fun before I'm an old woman. You don't have the backbone to stand up and make a man of yourself, and you never will. You aren't even trying."

"And this—this—Tom—is a real man?" He spat out the name.

"Tom cares about me. He listens when I talk. He is all the things I want and you will never be," she cried.

"You make me sick!" he shouted. "First you con me into marrying you to win a bet. You sweet talk me into buying your dream house and I saddle myself with a big debt to try to make you happy. And this is the thanks I get for my trouble."

"Look," she said in a flat voice, "I was

planning to tell you soon. I don't love you anymore, and I do love Tom. Our living together any longer isn't being fair to either of us. Our marriage died a long time ago. I have an appointment with an attorney next week. I plan to divorce you as soon as possible."

John stared at her. She had spoken as calmly as if she were planning a trip to the zoo. He knew she meant every word. He sat down slowly and put his head in his hands.

"I'm sorry," she said in quiet finality. "Honestly, I am. I don't hate you. I just don't love you anymore. All I ask is that you make it easy for both of us. We'll both be better off as soon as this mess is settled."

John cursed and whirled about. In giant strides he reached the door, went out, and slammed the door behind him.

Chapter 23

How he got through the rest of the day, John could never recall. He had no idea what to expect in the evening. Would Lynette take what he had said when he left as an order to leave? Would she be gone? Would she take Todd with her? *Todd! Where was he when I was home? Surely he would have come or called if he had heard me talking. He couldn't have slept through all that noise. I must know where he is!*

Frantic with fear, John called the babysitter. "Is Todd there?" he asked as soon as Judy answered.

"Yes." She sounded puzzled at the unusual call. "Lynette brought him early today."

"Is he all right?"

"Yes, he's all right. Was he sick?"

"No," John answered quickly, relief flooding his voice. "Just checking." He hung up abruptly.

Never had he been so glad to see his son as he was that evening. He swooped the child into his arms, nearly squeezing the breath out of him. Todd laughed and wriggled to be let down. John thought he could not bear to let him out of his sight for a second. Todd had become immeasurably precious in a single afternoon. Let Lynette have the house and anything she wanted if she left; only Todd must he have. He would never let her take Todd away.

The two went home as usual. Todd was mercifully unaware of the upheaval in his home. The familiar normalcy of the moment renewed John's lagging spirits and gave him hope. Perhaps it was all a bad dream.

He expected the house to be empty, for Lynette was usually at work at this time of the day. A note was propped against the napkin holder as it often was. He snatched it up and scanned it quickly. There was no salutation.

"Since you know about Tom," he read, "there is no use pretending any longer. I will not be back. You will hear from my attorney soon."

No signature was given or needed. The

small gold circlet left under the note spoke silent volumes.

The cautiously hopeful feeling he had nurtured on the way home shattered. His heart dropped like a stone to the bottom of a lake. There had been no mistake. It was not a dream, not even a cruel joke. She was gone. She really meant to divorce him. She had tossed him aside as easily as if he were a worn-out garment. She had no need, no use for him any longer. The rejection stung painfully.

Todd, impatient for his supper, tugged at his father's hand. "Daddy, le's eat supper," he lisped.

"Yes, sugar lump," John said absently. "Daddy will get supper."

Vacantly, he examined the contents of the refrigerator. He closed it again without removing anything. One cupboard after another was opened and closed. He did not know what he saw or even what he was looking for.

Who feels like eating? I couldn't get one thing past this lump in my throat. The sight of food makes me sick.

Nauseated, he dumped some cold cereal in a bowl and poured milk over it. He plopped Todd on his chair and pushed the bowl in front of him. "Eat that," he commanded shortly.

I've got to find out where Lynette went, he thought desperately. *I didn't mean she should leave. Is she with this Tom—whoever he is? I don't even know the guy's last name. Maybe she's at work.*

Wildly, he called her supervisor to see if she had reported for work. She had not. Neither had she given any reason for her absence, nor had she given a notice of termination.

Maybe she went home to her parents. That must be it.

But the call to his mother-in-law also resulted in a dead end.

"No, she isn't here," Mrs. Eisleman said in answer to John's question and explanation. "I'm sorry this happened. But if things had been different over there, she would not have done this. I know she has been terribly disappointed in you, and I'm not surprised to hear she left."

John flinched at the blow of the words. She was obviously placing the blame on him.

"Who has Todd?" Mrs. Eisleman asked. "Who will raise the kid now?"

"I have him, and I'll raise him," John replied firmly.

As he replaced the phone, John could only conclude Lynette had gone off with this Tom fellow. No one knew what had become of her. It was apparently more than an overnight trip, for many of her clothes and cosmetics were gone, he discovered. Miserably, he called Judy and asked if she would be able to keep Todd all day.

"Yes, I can do that. Lately he's been here most of the day quite often," she said.

"I see," John emphasized each word separately.

The last thing he felt like doing was to go to work. But he had to go whether he wanted to or not. There was very little sleep for him that night. Frightening questions without answers tumbled over each other in his mind. Without his wife's paycheck, how could he meet the mortgage payments? If she got a divorce, would she be able to claim any of the property? Would she sue for custody of Todd? Would alimony payments be added to his debts? It was too much to think about. He would take each day as it came. Of only two things was he sure. He would never give up Todd, and he would sell the house if she filed for divorce. He did not know where he would go, but he would not keep on working to pay for a fine house he had bought only to please a woman who no longer wanted him or it.

For the present, he would do nothing. He

would simply wait to see what developed. Perhaps she would change her mind and come back. She had not taken all of her things, after all. That gave him a little hope.

But do I want her if she does come back? Could I ever forget what she did? I don't know, he thought wearily. *I don't even know what I want myself.*

I've got to pull myself together for Todd's sake, he told himself in the morning. He got ready for work early and walked aimlessly through the house, wishing it were time to go. He loathed this house and what it had done to him. He had to get out of it. Softly, he stepped into the nursery. Todd was already awake. He jumped up as soon as he saw John and stretched out his little arms to be lifted out of the crib.

"Well, young man. Are you awake already?" The happy little face cheered him momentarily. "Come. Let's get you dressed. You're going bye-bye."

"Bye-bye," Todd repeated happily. "Daddy go bye-bye."

"Daddy must go to work," John explained. "You are going to Judy's house today."

Todd was too small to ask any questions about his mother's absence and the change in the daily schedule. But he was aware of it. Likewise, he asked no questions when John brought his clothes and put them in the closet of the nursery. John knew he could never bear to go into his and Lynette's bedroom again. The intrusion of a third person into what was rightfully theirs alone was so revolting that it demolished his pleasant memories.

And that is the superman who is all the things I am not? he thought in wry disgust. *Where are Lynette and this guy now? What are they doing?* He could picture them together. *He can't have anything I don't have.*

The next two days were an ordeal. Later, John remembered little of what happened. It took concentrated effort to remember even simple things. When he left work he wandered through the parking lot, searching for his car. He could not remember where he had parked. He ate almost nothing and slept very little. He could not think clearly. He watched every passing car and pedestrian, hoping to catch sight of Lynette. Yet, he could not have explained why he watched or what he would do if he should see her. Those he met every day at work knew something was wrong. But to tell someone Lynette had left him would make it too real. Keeping it to himself somehow seemed to prevent it from becoming stark reality.

"Hey, man!"

John turned slowly as Joe came flying down the steps into the incinerator room. His sharp voice cut through the fog that surrounded John's muddled mind. "Have you gone deaf? I called you three times."

"Sorry," John apologized. "I didn't hear you."

"Open that door," Joe pointed as he grabbed a hose. "This thing is pouring out black smoke. You know that's illegal. Who taught you to run this thing anyway?"

John shrugged. "Mike."

Joe swore. "Whatsa matter with you? The last coupla days you're walking around here like you're half asleep. Did ya fight with your wife?"

"Sort of."

"Well, kiss and make up. Give her candy and flowers and get over it."

"How am I going to give her candy and flowers when I don't know where she is?" John asked dully.

"You don't know . . ." Joe's voice died away. Suddenly he understood. "You mean your wife left you?" he asked more softly.

"Yeah. She left me. Ran off with some rich guy." It was out. To hear the ugly words stripped him naked of all dignity and self-esteem.

"I see," Joe was pensive. "That explains a lot of things. That's rotten luck. Sorry to hear it."

John's eyes stung with tears at the sympathy Joe offered. He shrugged as if it did not matter and turned back to the incinerator.

"I've been thinking," Joe said as he came back about an hour later. "You have two weeks of vacation coming. You could have it now. I'll bend the rules and let you take your vacation, beginning tomorrow if you want it."

What good will that do? John thought indifferently.

"You're really not fit to work," Joe pressured.

"All right," John agreed. "I'm losing my mind, and I must keep my head on straight for Todd's sake."

What will I do for two whole weeks? he wondered in the midnight hours. He regretted now that he had agreed to take his vacation. *What was I thinking? I'll go stark, raving mad if I'm cooped up in this house for two weeks. If it were summer we could find things to do. But there's nothing to do in January.*

Sleep, when it came, was brief and fitful. Light filtered through the drapes and touched John's face softly. *Something is wrong*, he thought as he began to waken. *I don't remember what it is. I don't want to know.* He dozed again. Slowly waves of consciousness broke again. *Something is terribly wrong*, he thought again as he once again began to surface. *I don't want to know what it is. I don't want to wake up.* He relaxed, willing his mind to vacancy. The cycle was repeated tormentingly every few minutes until at last Todd's calls brought John to full consciousness.

Full recollection hit him like a bucket of ice water. *I must get up. Todd is awake. I'm the only one here. Lynette is gone. Lynette and Tom. Where are they? She's probably in his arms right this minute. I don't want to get up. I can't go on.*

"Daddy, Daddy," Todd continued to call.

John dragged himself off the sofa and shuffled heavily to the nursery. Even Todd's happy face failed to cheer him. *How am I ever going to make it?* he thought wretchedly. *How can I be both father and mother to my son? He's so little. He can't grow up right without a mother.*

"Mama bye-bye," Todd said as John lifted the little fellow out of the crib.

"Yes, Mama is bye-bye," John agreed as a knife turned in his heart. *She's bye-bye all right. If he knew how much she is bye-bye*

. . . Poor little kid. He doesn't even know she doesn't want him anymore. How can a mother desert her own child? Mom would never have done that. I wish I could go back and be a boy again. My troubles were so small then they could be mended on Mom's lap. I never knew how good I had it at home. Oh! I want to go home, his heart cried with a fierce longing.

Why not? The question startled him momentarily. *Lynette can't stop me. I'm on vacation. I'm free to go home if I want to. I'm going to go.*

Chapter 24

Acting on impulse, John went to the telephone and dialed his parents' number. He waited impatiently while it rang. He could picture someone going to answer it. *Maybe they're not home.* His excitement died and then revived when he heard it being picked up and his father's voice answering.

"Pop, this is John," he identified himself.

"John!" Pop's voice showed both pleasure and surprise. "Good to hear from you. How is everybody out there?"

John thought carefully. How should he answer?

"I'm sure Todd is growing up fast," Pop commented when John did not speak.

"Yes." His mind was suddenly blank. He did not know what to say.

Pop waited. The silence deepened. "Are

you still there?" he asked.

"Yes."

Silence.

"Is something wrong, John?" Pop's voice was puzzled.

"Yes."

Silence.

"Do you want to tell me about it?"

"I don't know."

"Why did you call?"

"I don't remember."

"John! Are you all right?" Pop's voice had a sharp edge of alarm. "Something is wrong. Is Lynette there?"

"No."

"Where is she?"

"I don't know."

"What do you mean? Where did she go?"

"With Tom."

"Tom who?"

"I don't know. Some rich guy."

"John, what are you saying? Are you telling me Lynette left you?"

"Yes. She went with Tom." His head felt heavy and stupid.

"Where is Todd?"

"Here with me."

"What are you going to do?"

"I don't know."

"Aren't you working today?"

That's it! Now I remember. "They told me to take my two weeks of vacation. I thought maybe I'd come to see you."

Pop thought rapidly. John sounded like he needed help. "Can you stay for two weeks?"

"I don't know."

"John, you sound confused. I don't have anything to do today that can't wait. If you want me to, I can come and bring you home. Should I?"

"It doesn't matter."

"I believe I will then. Mom and I will both come. All right?"

"If you want to."

"We'll leave as soon as we can," Pop promised as he hung up.

Norman turned from the telephone and looked into his wife's anxious eyes. "We'll have to go to John right away," he told her.

Ida's eyes held his gaze. Foreboding of trouble flecked them with fear. "What's wrong?" She spoke quickly.

"Lynette left him."

"Oh, no!"

"He sounds like he's about to have a nervous breakdown. He wants to come home. He said he has two weeks of vacation. I think we'll go get him and try to keep him here at least that long."

"Where's Todd?"

"John has him, but I'm sure he isn't in shape to take care of him. Can you go along to bring them home?"

Ida untied her apron and nodded. "I'll get ready right away."

The morning inched endlessly along. John had to hunt for everything he wanted. He could not remember where the sugar bowl was kept. He opened and closed the refrigerator door three times until he remembered it was the milk he wanted. He felt as though he had accomplished a major task when he finally had Todd fed and dressed. Wearily, he sank into a stuffed chair, slouched and rested his head against the back of the chair. He was so tired. The wedding portrait Lynette had placed on the mantel when they moved into the house was directly in his line of vision. He stared at it. He needed no portrait to remember their wedding.

He crossed the room and picked it up. He stood, his eyes riveted on the two faces that smiled up at him. *How young and ignorant I was!* Mentally, he travelled back to the day he and Lynette had become one "until death do us part." He relived the magical honeymoon days and each experience that slowly had constructed a wall of mistrust and disillusionment between them. Painfully, he compared the sweet, almost shy girl he had thought she was the day the portrait was taken with the woman she was now. He had assumed she would be the kind of wife and mother he had been taught women should be. Of course their home would be different in some ways than his parents' had been. He had known that and had no regrets about it. He had not been sure then he could ever be happy with a home like the one in which he had been raised. He had seen too much of the way other people lived. One did not need to be a Mennonite to be a Christian. Mennonites had too many rules about things not directly related to salvation, he had thought.

He knew now, though it was too late, he had not known the real Lynette. The person he had thought she was on their wedding day did not exist. That person had merely been a part she was playing to "get" him. The romance had rushed headlong into marriage without their taking time to learn to truly know each other. Neither one had fulfilled the expectations of the other.

A little over three years ago we were married for "as long as we both shall live." And now she says our marriage is dead. Is this the corpse I'm looking at? If it is, I ought to give it a funeral. But I can't do that. When a thing is buried it is gone. I can't believe our marriage is over. It's not dead, only in trouble. If I can find out where she is, I'll ask her to go with me to a marriage counselor. We can work things out and begin again. I'll find another job, do anything she wants if she'll only come back.

He returned the portrait to its place on the mantel. His daydream of a better future acted as a euphoriant, temporarily eliminating the anguish of reality. His parents' arrival returned him to the present.

"Where are your things?" Mom asked after their greetings had been exchanged.

"Things?" John did not know what she meant.

"Didn't you pack any clothes or anything?"

"Oh! No."

"That's all right," Mom assured him. "If you tell me where the things are, I'll pack them."

"We want you to come and stay as long as you can," Pop added. "You'll need to bring some things along."

"I didn't think of that," John apologized feebly as he led the way to the nursery.

They found the drawers were nearly empty. He had not done any laundry for nearly a week. Mom stuffed all the dirty laundry into

239

a garbage bag to take home for washing. She thought of everything—coats, boots, mittens, some favorite toys for Todd. Pop turned down the heat and prepared the house for the time it would be vacant. It was a relief to have someone there to take charge and tell him what to do. John gladly rolled the responsibility onto the capable shoulders of his parents. With their help, the packing was soon finished.

"You sit in the front with Pop," Mom said as she opened the back door of the car. "Todd and I are going to get better acquainted here in the back on the way home."

Todd snuggled into his grandmother's lap and laid his head on her ample bosom. He had no memories of this grandma, but knew instinctively she loved him. Pop discreetly left John alone with his thoughts. Todd and Mom's cheerful chatter kept the trip from being completed in an awkward silence. Relieved of all responsibility, John slept.

In some ways, it was a comfort to be at home. John was freed from all responsibility and the need to make any decisions. It was a luxury to sit down to a meal without preparing it. But the food stuck in his throat. Todd was cared for without any effort on his father's part. He enjoyed the farm and animals immensely. He basked in all the attention he received. His twin aunts quickly spoiled him, granting every whim and desire.

Lynette was in John's thoughts continually. Over and over he relived their brief marriage, sorting out the causes for its disintegration. Regardless of which route his reasoning travelled, somehow the blame for the situation always seemed to rest on his side. Only in his dreams did happiness return. Then, Lynette was restored to the sweet, tender girl she had once been. Their love was real and satisfying. The pounding in his chest gave way to a consuming loneliness when he awoke to the reality of his surroundings and the emptiness of the other half of the bed. He lay awake until morning, tormented by speculations of what might have been.

Each morning was an obstacle to be hurdled. Many mornings he stayed in bed until nearly noon, simply because he had no ambition to get up. He spoke little and said nothing to anyone about the pain he was suffering. He was invited to attend church services with the family on Sunday morning, but when he refused, no pressure was applied. They understood he could not face the questions about Lynette that would surely be asked.

Marlin's two years of service in British Honduras were completed and the family was excitedly preparing for his return. The whole family, including Jane, Becky and Ken, and the grandchildren piled into a van to go to the airport to meet his flight. It was impossible for John to be unaffected by their excitement. He joined the welcoming party but could not enter fully into the spirit of the occasion.

Laughter, tears, hearty handclasps, and embraces enveloped Marlin as he reentered the family circle. They listened intently as he related some of his experiences on the homeward journey. Listening, John was aware of the vast difference Marlin's time of service had made in his life. He had left home two years ago, an inexperienced youth who had led a sheltered life. He was returning an adult man, tanned and broad-shouldered from the hard work he had done. But as he spoke, a more significant change became evident. His conversation reflected new thought patterns and goals for his life, revealing a spiritual growth that outdistanced the physical changes.

John envied Marlin. He could not help comparing Marlin's return to his own homecoming the week before. Marlin's future was bright with promise. His own looked hopeless.

The two weeks had passed as if in a dream. Nothing had been resolved in John's mind. He wished he could forget he had ever heard of Allendale and never return. But that was impossible. He must return, if for no other reason than to settle his financial affairs.

"We would be glad to keep Todd for awhile," Mom offered when the day came for them to leave. "It would save you the cost of a babysitter. You could spend weekends here with him."

John considered the offer only momentarily. There was and could be only one answer. "No, thanks," he refused. "I can't go home without him."

"I understand." Mom did not insist. "But if you change your mind anytime, let us know. We'll be glad to have him."

Ida had fallen totally and unashamedly in love with Todd during his stay. She held him on her lap as much as he would allow during the long drive back to Allendale. It hurt her to think of the motherless home at the end of the road. The impressionable first years were so vital in the molding of a life and passed so quickly. How could Todd develop properly in this situation? He needed the love and security of both a mother and father.

Mom and Pop stayed long enough to help John unpack and get settled again. Mom could not be persuaded to leave until she had set the house in order and helped John stock his shelves with groceries. She deposited a supply of quick meals and baked goods in his refrigerator and freezer. It was typical of the way she best expressed her affections. Gushy words and emotional displays did not come naturally. Her love wore practical working shoes.

"You really ought to find a good, Bible-believing church somewhere," Pop suggested when Mom was finally satisfied with her labors and they were ready to leave.

"I know," John admitted. "Lynette said we would send Todd to Sunday school when he is old enough to go. He could go to the nursery class now, but somehow we just never got started sending him."

"Don't *send* him, *take* him," Pop said gently.

"I guess I should." John hung his head.

After his parents had gone, John could not help but wonder if he had done the right thing in keeping Todd with him. The child would be cared for much better by his grandparents. He felt inadequate to be both father and mother to his son. Still, knowing his parents cared gave him strength to go on and try to do the impossible. Somehow he did not feel as completely forsaken as he had several weeks ago.

Chapter 25

After a fashion, life resumed. John returned to work in a slightly better frame of mind than before. The vacation time spent at home had restored some of his mental equilibrium. The turmoil that frothed inside was concealed by the calm exterior that was visible.

News of the separation had traveled in his absence. When he returned it was common knowledge. Every time he met someone he knew for the first time after his return, he sensed their thoughts were of his personal affairs. Though he could smile and be friendly, later he had a hard time remembering what they said unless it related to divorce or his situation. If the comment hurt or gave a ray of hope, he digested and redigested it.

"You're holding up so well through this,"

was a standard comment.

Is that a compliment or criticism? he wondered. *What do they expect me to do? A person doesn't die just by wishing they were dead. But if this is living, what is dying like?* Forcefully, he pushed the thought away. *I must live for Todd's sake.*

He had heard nothing from Lynette or her attorney since the day she left. Reasoning that "no news is good news," he nurtured a cautiously hopeful attitude. He could see she had been back in his absence, for more of her personal belongings were missing. But he had no idea where she was or how to get in contact with her. He longed to see her again to beg her forgiveness and ask her to come back. But he could do nothing as long as she maintained silence. He was always either consciously or subconsciously on the alert for the sight of a white Cadillac.

It was already dark when, several days after his return to Allendale, John heard a car come in the drive. Visitors were rare these days and he tensed. *What will I say or do if it's Lynette?* All the things he had wanted to say suddenly vanished into thin air.

The sound of the footsteps approaching the front door were firm and heavy, not the sound of a woman's footsteps. John relaxed slightly. When the doorbell rang, he opened the door to see a strange man on the porch.

"Mr. John B. Shenk?" the man questioned.

"Yes," John answered, stooping to pick up the small boy who had trailed him to the door.

"I am the sheriff," the stranger said, showing his credentials. "I am here to serve you with a copy of a complaint in divorce that has been filed at the courthouse by your wife, Lynette E. Shenk. You will need to sign here, please, to verify proof of service."

"Oh!" John paused. "Come in," he said woodenly.

He set Todd on the floor again, took the pen the sheriff extended and shakily signed his name at the indicated place.

"You have twenty days to respond," the sheriff explained quietly. "If you do not respond in that time a date will be set for the hearing. You will receive that notice by certified mail."

"Thank you," John said stiffly as the sheriff opened the door to leave. He fought a ridiculous urge to laugh as soon as the words were out of his mouth. *Thank you? Thanks for what? For bringing the death certificate of my marriage?*

He looked at the paper he held in his hand. The words swam before his eyes. His legs were suddenly too weak to support him. Slowly, he read and reread the information the document provided. It was no mistake. In black and white the paper shouted Lynette had filed for a divorce from him. It listed cruelty as the grounds for divorce. *Cruelty!* The word leaped out and threatened to strangle him. It dealt a death blow to his already badly fractured self-esteem. *What will people say? They'll think I was a brute.* The rejection of being left for another had inflicted pain enough. This charge added insult to injury.

For several days, John deliberated, trying to determine what his next move should be. After weighing the information and advice of both his friends and a lawyer, he decided the cruelty charges could be proven false and the proceedings stopped.

I'll call the lawyer tomorrow and make an appointment to file a counter claim, he decided.

The telephone was ringing as he unlocked the front door that afternoon. He shifted Todd onto one arm and picked up the instrument with the other hand.

"Hello."

"Where have you been?" John's knees turned to jelly when Lynette's voice spoke in his ear. He sat down quickly and set Todd on the floor. The accusing, complaining pitch of her voice irritated him. "I didn't think it mattered to you where I am," he said flatly.

"I thought maybe you skipped the country," she laughed nervously. "I was back a few times for some things, and it didn't look like anyone had been around."

"I noticed," he said disjunctively.

"What did you do? Go into hiding?" she pressed.

"I took two weeks of vacation and went home," he said irritably. "What's it to you?"

"Oh, never mind," she suddenly seemed not to care. "That isn't why I called. I need to talk to you about the divorce. May I come over?"

"I suppose so." *You'd think we are strangers. She talks as if she is company.*

"I'll come over right away then," she said.

"No," he said quickly. "Wait until later when Todd is in bed. I don't want to talk about something like that in front of him."

"He's too little to know the difference," she laughed. "But I'll wait if that's how you want it."

The air was charged with tension when Lynette entered the house. Both were self-consciously awkward. John did not rise to meet her. She let herself in and took a chair across from him.

"You were notified of the divorce suit?" she said unnecessarily when he did not speak.

"Yes."

"What are you planning to do?"

"You know as well as I that I never laid a hand on you in all my life," he protested without answering her question. "Why did you charge me with cruelty?"

"There are other kinds of cruelty," she said stiffly. "I'm not going to say you were a wife beater."

"I would have more grounds for divorce than you," he pointed out. "But I don't want a divorce. I'm going to file a counter claim and fight it. I think I can win."

"Don't do that," she pleaded. "Tom got his divorce last week. We want to be married as soon as I can get mine. The less fuss you make, the better it will be for everybody."

"Better for you, you mean," he argued. "What about me? What about Todd? He needs a mother."

"You can marry somebody else. I don't care."

John stared. "Can't we start over and try again?" he pleaded. "If we went to a marriage counselor, maybe we could work out our problems."

"It wouldn't work." She shook her head.

251

"I know I haven't given you the kind of life you want," he apologized. "But if you'll come back I'll get another job. I'll go to night school and get some training. I'll do anything you want if you'll just come back." There was a pathos in his voice.

"There was a time I would have considered that, but not now," she dissented. "I don't think I ever really loved you. Tom and I love each other in a way I never knew existed. He is all I'll ever want."

"You won't give me another chance?"

"No. I'm sorry if you're hurt, but I'm tired of being a slave. Even if you stop me from getting a divorce, I'll never come back to you."

Her words stripped him of every ounce of pride he had left. He could think of nothing to say.

"If you do not file a counter claim in twenty days or appear at the hearing, the divorce will be granted automatically. Will you do that for me?"

"Why should I?"

"If you contest the divorce, I will file for custody of Todd." Her voice was calm and deliberate.

John jumped up. His eyes grew large and then hard. "Are you crazy?" he shouted. "I'll never give up Todd."

"If I sue for custody, you will. Natural mothers are seldom denied custody of small children if they request it."

"You can't do that," he panted.

"I won't, if you don't contest the divorce," she bargained.

He dropped weakly back into his chair. She had him cornered, and they both knew it. "Is that a promise?" he asked huskily. "If I don't contest the divorce, you won't sue for custody?"

"It's a promise. I swear it," she said solemnly. "You may have Todd and the house and everything. I won't ask for my half of the property, or alimony. I only want to be set free."

"All right," he agreed, choking on a sob. "I won't contest the divorce."

"Thank you. I knew you would cooperate," she beamed as she stood up. "I'd like to take a few more of my things if you don't mind, and then I'll be going."

If I don't mind?! His heart lay rent and trampled under her words. Yet, those same words provoked him. "Take everything you own," he said harshly. "If this is the end you never need to come back again. Leave your house key, too. I don't want you sneaking in here anymore when I'm gone. Just go away and leave us alone."

The sarcasm in his words boomeranged back into his ears with her reply. "I'll be glad to," she said.

He sat woodenly while Lynette went from room to room collecting things. He made no move to help her or to stop her from taking anything she wanted.

"I guess that's everything," she said hesitantly when she had finished.

She was only a few feet away from him. Her fragrance teased his nostrils. He wanted to beg her again to change her mind. But he knew it was useless.

"So, I'll be going," she continued when he did not reply.

He ignored her. *What does she expect me to say, "So long, it's been good to know you"?*

She crossed the room and opened the door. "I put my key on the table."

He nodded but did not lift his eyes. He looked so dejected she felt a twinge of pity for him in spite of herself. She looked at him strangely and closed the door behind her.

He sat motionless until the sound of her car died away in the distance. She was gone forever. He did not have the strength to move. She had blackmailed him into agreeing to let her go. He felt as though he had just attended his own funeral.

Chapter 26

The twenty days passed and John did not respond to the divorce suit. He had no choice. If he did as Lynette asked, Todd was his. If he fought the divorce, he might have neither wife nor child.

Following through on his decision to sell the house, a realtor's "For Sale" sign greeted him every time he came to or left the house. It was a house and nothing more to him. The home was broken and would never be mended. He did not regret selling the house. He had not wanted it in the first place. It was Lynette's dream house, not his. The whole house was a monument to their shattered dreams. He wanted to avoid it as much as possible. As winter gave way to spring, it was easier to find things to do outside. John and Todd often spent hours watching and feeding the ducks on the pond across town. They went for long walks and passed many evenings on the swings and in the sandbox at the playground in town. John hunted excuses to leave the house. It held too many reminders of happier times.

Contact with his parents had become more regular and frequent than at any time since John had first left home. He could sense his parents' concern for him and Todd, and he appreciated it. Unconsciously he began to lean on their opinions in the decisions he needed to make. Todd was always eager to visit the farm, and John needed no urging to make weekend trips. It was comforting to know the folks at home were praying for him, even though he did not pray himself.

When the certified letter arrived which notified him of the date of the hearing, he looked at it briefly and dropped it in the wastebasket. It was not important.

I'm not going, so it doesn't make any difference to me when the hearing is.

Yet, he was not entirely satisfied with his decision. In his childhood and youth he had always been taught divorce and remarriage is sin. But he had never thought about it very much. Now that he was involved in the situation, he did not know for sure what was right or wrong. It was no use to ask his parents, for he knew what they would say.

Before it's too late and the hearing is over, I've got to talk to somebody about this, he thought with anxiety. *Maybe it would help to talk to a minister. The only one I know here is the one that married us and baptized Todd. I'm ashamed to ask him for help, no more often than we went to church. But I've got to talk to someone.*

Reverend Lind was solicitous and affable when John arrived at the time appointed for the visit. He briefly outlined the situation and the questions that troubled him. "Am I doing the right thing to let her go and not contest the divorce?" he asked earnestly.

"I can understand your feelings," the pastor sympathized. "I hear so much of this kind of heartache these days. Many people come to me with this problem. It is always a difficult experience when a marriage dies. You are right that God's original plan was for one man and one woman to be married for life. But people found that concept illogical in many cases. Moses made allowance for divorce and remarriage in the law. There are times when it is best for everyone involved if the marriage is terminated. There are various reasons and causes for this. Sometimes when people marry young, they don't con-

257

sider what they are doing very carefully. Maybe you can see that in your decision to marry Lynette."

"But I loved her so much then and I was sure she loved me," John protested.

"I'm sure you did," the pastor assured him soothingly. "She may have been the right one for you at that time. But both of you have changed since then, haven't you? As you look back over the past three years, can you see how your values and goals may be changing from what they were when you were first married?"

"Yes, I can," John agreed thoughtfully.

"That's just the point," the pastor continued. "As we mature, we grow out of relationships. You and Lynette have been growing in different directions. Continuing your marriage, when you have grown so far apart, would hamper the development of your personality as well as hers. As people mature, they tend to grow into new relationships that better fit them at their stage of development."

"Then you are saying I should let Lynette go?" John asked.

"It isn't easy, I know. But it might be best for both of you," Reverend Lind said gently.

"But Todd needs a mother," John objected. "How can I raise a boy without a mother?"

"That need not be a permanent condition. In time you will probably remarry," the pastor stated.

"I could never marry another woman," John objected.

"You may feel that way now. You hurt deeply and are not ready to think of finding a new wife. But after a year or two, you will be very lonely. Somewhere you may meet a lovely woman who can fill God's plan for your developing personality. Then you will feel differently than you do today," the pastor smiled knowingly.

"But according to the Bible, wouldn't it be adultery for me to marry again as long as Lynette is living?" John asked.

"Oh, I know people used to believe that way years ago," Reverend Lind admitted. "But just as scientists have made advances and new discoveries in the past years, so has the clergy come to a fuller understanding of the Bible. Because the marriage vows are broken, you are no longer bound by them. You are the innocent party since you are not the one responsible for breaking the vows. You are free to remarry.

"God made man with the need for a woman," the pastor continued after a moment. "She supplies what he lacks and vice versa. It is God's plan for a man to desire a woman's love. Because God gave you that need, He surely does not expect you to live the rest of your life with those needs unfulfilled. He promised not to send us more trouble than we are able to bear. Then He went one step further and promised to make a way of escape so we will be able to bear it. That way of escape may well be in the form of another woman."

John sat silently for a few moments digesting Reverend Lind's words.

The pastor came around the desk and laid a hand on the shoulder of the troubled young man who had come to him for counsel. "I am here to help people," he said warmly. "Believe me, I know exactly how you feel. I went through the same thing myself ten years ago. I know now God allowed it to happen so I would be able to help people like you. God is blessing my ministry in a way that would not have been possible if I had not suffered the painful experience of divorce. My second wife and I have a wonderful marriage and great joy neither of us experienced in our first marriages. I believe God has some wonderful things for you, too, in the years ahead. You can trust Him to work it out for you."

"Thank you," was the only reply John

could formulate.

"I hope you are feeling better," the pastor said as John stood up.

"You have given me a lot to think about," John said honestly as he shrugged on his light jacket. *But I'm more confused than ever,* he thought to himself.

"Feel free to come back any time you have more questions or if you only need a listening ear," the pastor invited. "I'm always glad to be of service."

John nodded in reply and left the pastor's study. As good as they had sounded at the time, the pastor's answers were somehow too glib and compact. They were the exact opposite of what John had been taught. His temples pounded with the outbreak of an intense headache. Reverend Lind's counsel was disappointing and somehow nauseating.

Three years ago we made vows for life before Reverend Lind. Now that same man says those vows don't mean anything. Who or what is right? he wondered as he drove back to pick up Todd at the babysitter's.

A loud honking behind him startled him to attention. He was half way over the center line—and on a steep curve at that! He veered sharply back over the line, well over on his side of the road. The blood pounded in his ears. His head throbbed. *I'd better watch the road!*

On a level stretch, the car pulled up alongside him and the driver shouted, "That's a good way to end it all, buddy, if that's what you want." He smiled sarcastically and shot past John, on down the road.

"End it all." That's what he said. A good way to end it all. Maybe that would be best. I could save myself and a lot of other people a good deal of trouble if I just ran head-on into that tree up ahead. It looks good and solid. If I hit it at 90 mph, no one would ever know what happened. That would end all my problems. But what then? I'm not ready to die. Suicide would only add murder to my long list of sins. And what would happen to Todd? He needs me. I have to go on living if I want to or not.

The day of the hearing arrived, and John was painfully aware of it. But, bound by his promise, he stayed away. Nothing except his determination to keep Todd would have kept him away. He went to work as usual but moved in an absentminded daze. He tried to picture the scene in the courthouse and what was happening there. He imagined the accusations that were being leveled against him. He was humiliated to think of it. Those he met as he went mechanically about his duties never guessed the cold hand of desolation that squeezed his heart and mind to life-lessness.

"Don't you know what's happening?" he wanted to scream at the smiling faces around him. "My wife is divorcing me today. My life is falling apart and I can't do anything about it. Don't smile like that! If one more person says, 'Nice day, isn't it?' I'll screech!"

His mind raced on all day. In desperate futility he imagined the judge denying the divorce. It was the only hope. Yet, he knew it would undoubtedly be granted since he was not there to contest it. Somehow it just did not seem real that while he went about his work, others could be murdering his marriage. He became so confused he was really sure of nothing. His conflicting thoughts could not be controlled, and neither could he keep them from his mind.

The arrival of the certified letter several days later dispelled the mists of unreality and brought him cruelly face to face with the naked truth. The divorce had been granted; he knew it without opening the envelope. He delayed opening it until after Todd had been put to bed for the night. Then, with trembling hands, he slit the envelope and drew out the paper that informed him of the bitter fact. His hand shook so that he could scarcely read the words.

He sat, staring into space, aware of nothing around him. *What God hath joined together, let no man put asunder.* The words of the pastor at their wedding rang in his ears. If it was God who joined them, did God have anything to do with this paper? If man could put them asunder, had God really joined them together? *This is like going around in a circle and coming to your own tracks in the snow.*

He reached for his pack of cigarettes without being conscious of the action, lit one and sat taking long, desperate puffs. He lit another as soon as the first one was finished. Momentarily his mind was sidetracked by watching the smoke float lazily away.

Life is like that smoke, his contorted thoughts mocked him. *Yesterday I had a wife, today I don't. Here today, gone tomorrow. Nothing lasts forever. Why was I fool enough to think Lynette was mine forever? If I could have seen where I am today when I first started to slide . . . I thought then I could stop any time I wanted to. But I was having so much fun I didn't want to stop. Now I do and I can't. I'm trapped! I don't know how to find my way out of this mess. I'm lost. Lost!*

Listlessly, he folded the paper and returned it to the envelope. His hand stopped in mid-motion. He stared mesmerized by the gold band that encircled the third finger of his left hand. Painfully, he remembered when Lynette's slim fingers had slipped it on his finger. The circle was supposed to symbolize her unending love for him. The vows she had made then were broken. She said now she never loved him at all. She had not meant it even when she vowed it. How foolish to think that little gold band would keep her bound to him for life!

He tugged at the plain gold band. *If we aren't married anymore there's no point in wearing this ring.* It came off more easily than he had expected. He held it in the palm of his hand for a moment. Now that it was off, he did not know what to do with it. He had no use for it. *I might as well throw it away.* But somehow, he did not think he wanted to do that, for it symbolized a happier time. He would put his ring in the same place he had put hers. *At least the rings can be together*, he thought morbidly. Slowly he forced himself to ascend the stairs. He would have to go into their bedroom to get the little jewelry box. He had not been in that room since he had moved his things into the nursery with Todd.

With clammy hands, he opened the door,

switched on the light and stepped inside. Revulsion hit him at the sight of the bed. Something seemed to snap inside his head. He rushed to the dresser, jerked open the drawer and drew out the little box. He snatched Lynette's ring and raced out of the room, slamming the door behind him. He ran, panting, to the edge of his property, drew back and with a mighty thrust of his arm, threw the rings as far as he could. There was no sound, not even a faint tinkle to tell him where they had landed. He stood for a moment, listening to the silence. Then he slowly turned and shuffled back to the house.

Already he regretted the hasty action. He flexed his unadorned ring finger. It felt bare and looked as strange and empty as his heart felt. The loss of the rings seemed to signal the final end of their marriage. But he had lost more than the rings. He had lost part of himself. He knew he would never be able to find the rings again, nor would he ever again be a complete person.

Chapter 27

Lynette kept her bargain with John. He had not contested the divorce and she had not filed for custody of Todd or asked for any part of the property or alimony. The divorce was all she wanted and all she got. John was thankful for that. He knew she could have legally forced him into greater financial crisis. In that respect he had gotten off easy. But even that fact had a bitter taste. He knew she had not asked for a cent of his money only because she did not need it. Tom could well afford to support the extravagant lifestyle she wanted. She was gone and living in high style while he struggled along still paying her credit card bills and debts that littered the highway of their short marriage.

John watched the marriage license listings

daily, waiting and yet not really wanting to see Lynette's license listed. True to her word, she did not wait long after the divorce was final to remarry. The information printed with the marriage license listing told him her new husband was Thomas A. Leisawitz. He was 43 years old and lived in Martinsburg, West Virginia.

John could not help but wonder about the former Mrs. Leisawitz. Though he had never met her, he felt somehow a kinship with her and what she must be feeling. She had been rejected too, not for someone richer, but for someone younger. Did the Leisawitzes have any children? How many? How old were they? How were they faring emotionally? Or had the marriage and home been floundering for years before it fell apart so that they did not care? Perhaps Mrs. Leisawitz had already remarried too.

It hurt to know there was absolutely no hope of any reconciliation or change of heart. Lynette's heart belonged to another and soon, if not already, she would bear another man's name. He had no claim on her legally or otherwise. Except for the memories of what had been, the pain he now suffered, and Todd, it was as though their marriage had never been.

Several potential buyers had gone through

the house. The last couple seemed more interested in it than any previous ones. John was impatient to be rid of the house and the debt that went with it. He cut the price to encourage the sale. The buyers agreed and an agreement was signed. He was glad he had taken the advice of his attorney and gotten Lynette to sign legal papers relinquishing any right to her share of the property before the divorce. He could go ahead now and sell it without having to consult or see her. A settlement date was set for two months after the date of the agreement.

John began to be able to think ahead and formulate a few plans for the future. What was done was over and past. He could not change it. But he had to keep living and raise his son the best he could. He decided to move back home to be near his parents. A grandmother was the next best thing to a mother for Todd. He would accept his mother's offer to keep Todd during the day while he worked. He would find a small place somewhere nearby for the two of them. The sooner he could get away from Allendale and go back home, the sooner he could forget the past and begin a new life.

All his plans took a nosedive when he came home from work one day to find a white Cadillac parked in the drive. *Lynette!*

It can't be! His senses reeled as he got out of his car.

"What are you doing here?" he demanded coldly as she got out of her car and came to meet him.

"I have come for Todd," she said bluntly.

John stared. "You—What?!" His voice rose with the question.

"I want Todd and I've come to get him," she repeated.

"You may want him all right, but you're not going to get him," he said through clenched teeth. "You said I could have him."

"When did I say that?" She acted innocent.

"You know. You swore I could have Todd and all the property in exchange for the divorce. I let you go. You got what you wanted. I got Todd. He's mine!" John panted.

"I am still his mother even if I'm not your wife," she pointed out in a sticky-sweet voice. "I think we should do what is best for Todd. I can take care of him much better than you can. There's more where this came from." She waved her hand to indicate the car and her expensive pantsuit.

"You and your filthy money!" John exploded. "I may not have all that, but I love Todd and you don't. You never really wanted him. You don't want him now. You just want to torment me."

"I'm not thinking of you or myself." She controlled her voice with effort. "I'm thinking of what is best for Todd. Tom misses his own children. He wants to take Todd and raise him as his own. I see you sold the house. What are you going to do now?"

"None of your business," John answered rudely. "What I do and where I go has nothing to do with you."

"But Todd is my business," she argued hotly. "And I'd bet my bottom dollar I know what you are going to do. You're going to go back where you came from and give him to your wonderful mother. She'll raise him to be a good little ignorant Mennonite. I want my son to have a good education and a successful career. You're not going to make a Mennonite out of *my* son."

"Get off my property," he hissed fiercely. "Get out of here before I strangle your delicate little neck. I don't ever want to see you again."

"I'll go." She spun on her heel. "I'll go directly to an attorney and file for custody."

"You swore you wouldn't!" John cried.

"Prove it," she flung over her shoulder as she leaped into the car, slammed the door, and gunned it down the driveway.

271

Only now did John realize Todd was crying. *Poor kid! He's scared to death.* He never remembered what he did or said. But somehow he quieted Todd and got into the house. He sank lifelessly into a chair. His face was haggard, and he felt as if all the life had been drained from him. His legs were suddenly too weak to support him. He sat, staring straight ahead, seeing nothing. Then his gaze focused on their wedding portrait sitting in its place on the mantel. His fierce rage returned, replacing the temporary lethargy of shock.

Why did I ever let that thing there? he thought savagely. In a flash he crossed the room, picked up the picture and threw it against the wall. The glass splintered and scattered at his feet.

Todd stared and screamed. "Daddy! Daddy!"

John reached blindly into the jagged fragments, prying with his fingers at the edge of the picture. The sharp glass cut a gash in his finger. Blood spurted across the faces of the smiling couple under the broken glass. heedlessly, he clawed the picture from the wreckage of its frame, tore it in two, and crumpled the pieces into a ball.

"Daddy!" Todd screamed again, pulling frantically at his father's leg. He had never seen his father so angry and violent. The sight of the blood streaming across his father's hand terrified him.

John fumbled for the handkerchief in his pocket and clumsily wound it around the gash in his finger. Todd's screams jerked him back to some semblance of sanity. He felt like screaming and crying with his son, but instead forced himself to speak comforting, calming words. Slowly he set about the business of bandaging his finger properly, cleaning up the mess and trying to act normal for Todd's sake. He remembered now he had not put the picture away because he had not wanted Todd to completely forget his mother. Suddenly now, he wanted Todd to forget her, and the sooner the better.

One minute he could not quite believe Lynette would actually file for custody after she had so solemnly sworn not to. But the next minute he knew she very well might. She had lied and broken her word so often before, why wouldn't she now? He silently cursed himself for not getting their agreement in writing. It was a matter of her word against his if it came to court.

I'll fight her to the teeth if she files for custody. He clenched his fists and waved them at the empty air. *Over my dead body! She'll get him over my dead body!*

273

The days dragged by endlessly. Lynette's threats hung like a hangman's noose over his head, ready to slip down at any moment and suffocate him. The thought of filing for legal custody himself tempted him, but he knew that was more dangerous than no action. Natural mothers were seldom denied custody of small children. The court would certainly take her new husband's income into consideration. Matched against his income, John knew he had a slim chance of winning if the case came to a hearing. He waited, hoping and willing himself to believe she had discarded her threats when her anger had cooled.

The sky was painted in soft hues of the gold and pink of an early summer sunset as John romped beneath the trees with Todd behind the house. His troubles pushed out of sight for the moment, John trotted around the lawn, giving Todd a "horsey ride" to an accompaniment of shrieks of delight. He slowed abruptly when he turned to see someone standing at the corner of the house observing them. There was something vaguely familiar about the man. Slowly he jogged toward the stranger, his eyes stamped with question marks.

"Nice evening, isn't it?" the stranger said, extending a hand as John neared.

"Yes, it is," he agreed automatically, swinging Todd down from his shoulders to the grass.

"I'm Sheriff Johnson," the man introduced himself. "I have come to deliver to you a copy of the custody suit that has been filed at the courthouse." He held out an envelope.

John stood transfixed. He turned deathly white and swayed as if struck.

"I'm sorry," the sheriff said gently. "This is a part of my job I don't enjoy, but I have to do my duty." John nodded dumbly. "You have twenty days to respond to this suit. You will be notified by mail of the date of the hearing."

With a shaking hand, John accepted the proffered envelope. He said nothing.

"I'm sorry," the sheriff repeated, looking from John to Todd and back again. He turned and disappeared around the corner of the house.

Bitterness and anger churned inside John, tying his stomach in a hard knot. Methodically, he put Todd to bed. Then he opened the bar and poured a stiff shot of whiskey for himself. How long he sat, seething and drinking, he did not know. He mentally rehearsed what he might say at the hearing. He would tell the judge how he was tricked into marrying Lynette and she had borne the

275

child to him for selfish reasons. He would prove she had never really wanted or loved Todd. He would bar no holds at the hearing. Every nasty thing he could think of against her, he would say. Surely the judge would put some value on the worth of love.

In the morning, he lost no time in making arrangements to file a countersuit. He would fight with every ounce of strength and every cent it took to gain custody of his son. When he called his parents to give them the news, they sympathized with him and pledged their prayers as he had known they would.

The hearing was set for a week before the final settlement of the sale of the house. For months John had felt as though his emotions were walking a tightrope. Just when he had begun to feel cautiously optimistic, this new jolt had thrown him down again to begin all over. He battled through the feelings again of denial, anger, bitterness, and despair in an unending circle.

The days he managed fairly well. It was the nights that were long and torturous. He slept fitfully. Often he awoke in the middle of the night, sopping wet with perspiration. Then he sought escape through drink. A stiff shot of whiskey always numbed his tortured mind. But in the morning he came back to reality and the same problems. Yet, under the strain of the pending custody case, he came regularly to the bar every night. Each time, the amount he cunsumed was more than the night before. It was his crutch to get him through until morning. He wished he could pray, but he could not. He had wandered away from God too many years. God would not hear. He had brought all these problems upon himself. Now he was being smothered by the curtain of his own carelessness.

Chapter 28

Slowly and deliberately, setting one foot in front of the other, John trudged up the steps of the courthouse. His stomach was tied in knots. The decision of the judge this morning would determine Todd's future. Side by side with his determination to fight for custody was a sense of foreboding. He was counting heavily on the judge's consideration of the intangibles of love, acceptance, and self-esteem that he was able to give his son against the advantages of affluence Lynette would present as the argument in her favor.

Like the strangers they now were, John and Lynette sat stiffly across from each other as they waited for their case to be called. It was almost a relief to go into the chamber before the judge. The hearing was conducted in an informal atmosphere. John, Lynette, and their respective attorneys each presented their side of the argument. John felt degraded to hear Lynette's opinion of him aired before these strangers. He was a lazy, good-for-nothing bum to hear her talk. He countered her attack by picturing her as an unnatural mother, more interested in herself and a good time than in the emotional and physical well being of her son. Attacks and counterattacks flew back and forth as each one tried to say the worst possible things about the other.

"This is one of the cases where it is very difficult for me to make a decision," the judge said at last. He paused and placed his fingertips together carefully.

John leaned forward slightly, tense and suddenly feeling cold and faint. In a matter of minutes the judge would announce his decision.

"Some custody decisions are easily made because one parent is clearly unfitted to care for the child properly," the judge continued. "But both of you have a convincing argument in your favor. I must make a decision for one and against the other. Either way, one of you will be unhappy. It's a part of my job that I wish I did not have to do. My decision must be based upon the needs of the child, his age, and other circumstances."

The judge paused again and leaned his chin upon his fingertips. He sat for what seemed like eons, staring and thinking. At last, he looked up. John held his breath. The moment had come.

"It is my decision that custody of the child in this case be awarded to the mother," he said.

John's heart stopped and then raced back into action. A dizzying blackness swam before his eyes. His head dropped in defeat and he squeezed his eyes shut to hold back the tears. Vaguely he heard the judge's explanation of his visiting rights and privileges. He was ordered to give Todd to Lynette the following day.

"I'll come to pick him up around ten tomorrow morning." Lynette could not hide the triumph in her voice when she spoke. "I'll expect you to have his things packed and ready to go."

John nodded dully without looking up. He could not trust himself to speak. He remained sitting woodenly after the others had risen to their feet, preparing to leave the chamber. With herculean effort he raised himself to his feet and started toward the door. There were no words of sympathy or expressions of understanding that could begin to comfort him.

Impatiently he raced to the baby-sitter to pick up Todd. He had less than 24 hours to spend with his son before he was taken away. He could not waste a second.

In one swift motion he scooped Todd up from the floor where he was playing and nearly squeezed the breath out of him. Judy's eyes met John's over Todd's head. She lifted her eyebrows in question. John pressed his lips tightly together and buried them in Todd's hair to hide their quivering. He shook his head in silent answer to the silent question.

"Oh! I'm sorry," Judy's voice was low and compassionate. "When?"

"Tomorrow," John said with a catch in his voice. "So I guess this is it. I'll pay you in full on payday."

"Don't worry about it," Judy tried to console him. "I'll really miss him."

Not half as much as I will, John's broken heart cried.

Time both dragged and flew as John gathered Todd's clothes and toys. It was worse than putting away the belongings of a deceased child, for this child tagged at his heels, chattering charmingly in his limited way. He felt as though he was preparing to send his son to a fate worse than death. He could not comfort himself with the thought that Todd was at peace and in the presence of God.

Anxious to learn of the outcome of the hearing, Ida called in the evening. She was almost as disappointed as John when he told her the results. She offered to come and stay with them but he refused. He did not want anyone else there, not even his own mother. He wanted Todd completely to himself.

Sleep eluded John that night. He rocked Todd to sleep and sat rocking long after the child was asleep. Only when his arms grew so tired he could hold his son no longer, did John finally lay him in the crib. Then he pulled the chair beside the crib and continued to sit, watching the sleeping child and thinking until he felt he was going insane. He considered running away and almost decided to do it. But common sense finally convinced him it was useless. It would only prolong the agony. Eventually Lynette would get Todd anyway. She had the law on her side. Running would only get him into more trouble. The less of a scene he made when she came for Todd, the better it would be for the child.

Wearily, he passed the back of his hand across his forehead and leaned back in the chair. There was no way out, nothing he could do. He was licked, beaten, finished. His mind raced on even as he dozed.

Morning brought renewed agony. He was painfully aware with every step of the routine that it was the last time he would dress Todd, the last breakfast he would give him, the last time for everything.

He's so little he won't even remember me, John's heart cried in anguish. *He'll grow up thinking that old Tom is his father.* He paced back and forth while Todd ate breakfast, trying to think of something to do so Todd would not grow up without any knowledge of his real father. His eyes fell on the 8x10 photo that had been taken of Todd when he was a year old. *A picture! That's it! I'll put a picture of myself in with Todd's things.* Fired by the idea, he searched his mind for just the right picture. *I've got it!* A sickly grin twisted his face.

He squatted, reached into the bottom of the buffet in the formal dining room and drew out a thick album of wedding photos he had hidden there. He flipped the pages swiftly and then chose one of Lynette and himself flanked by their parents. He tucked it carefully between some of the clothes near the bottom of the box. He knew, even as he did it, that Lynette might throw the picture away or keep it from Todd. *But if he ever does see it when he's old enough to ask questions, let her explain,* he thought bitterly.

It was a few minutes after ten when Lynette arrived. Carefully made up and smartly tailored, she approached the front door and touched the bell. Ashen and trembling, he opened the door. She stepped inside without being invited. He was suddenly infuriated at the sight of her. He knew if he uttered a word he would lose control completely. He flopped on a chair and stared at her wordlessly. She ignored him.

"Hi, sweetheart," she cooed to Todd, dropping on her knees and hugging him in a great show of affection. "Mommie came to take you bye-bye. Do you want to go bye-bye with Mommie? It's a little chilly. Do you have a jacket? Oh, here's one." She picked a red windbreaker off the top of the box of clothes John had set in the corner. "Come to Mommie, honey. Let's put your jacket on," she chattered nervously.

Todd stared at this strange woman with large, puzzled eyes and did not move. She reached for him and began to put on his jacket. He made no response. She turned to John. "I'm glad you are being sensible and prepared Todd for this. I'd hate to have a big scene."

John did not look up or answer. Seeing he was ignoring her, she began to carry Todd's things to the car. John made no move to help her. He would not give Todd to her, but neither could he prevent her from taking the boy. The law gave her that right. So he sat, rooted to the spot, acutely aware, but seemingly unconscious to what she was doing. Once, he moved to take Todd in his arms and smother him with kisses. But he restrained himself, knowing it would open the floodgates of his emotions. For Todd's sake he dared not let that happen.

After the last box had been stowed in the car, Lynette returned to the house and picked up Todd. "Okay, sweetheart," she cooed. "Mommie's ready. Now we'll go bye-bye."

Todd wriggled and reached for John. "Daddy!" His voice was edged with fear.

"No, no, honey," Lynette soothed. "He's not coming. Just you and Mommie this time. We'll go bye-bye and get you some candy." She kept talking as she went towards the door. "See. Mommie has some candy for you." She reached into the pocket of her dress suit and extracted a lollipop.

Todd was not to be bribed so easily. His quick mind perceived something greatly abnormal was taking place. He threw the lollipop across the floor and screamed, "No! I want Daddy!"

Lynette struggled with the kicking, squirming child as she made her way quickly to the car and locked him inside. Todd's howls increased to a frenzied volume and then gradually faded from his father's hearing as he was driven away.

Then there was nothing; not even the sound of crying. But still, John heard the screams that had been. *I want Daddy! I want Daddy!*

The anger that had been bottled up inside him for so long exploded in a blinding flash. *Of all the things she did to me, THIS IS THE WORST!* He jumped up and took a few angry strides across the room. He bumped into the recliner and stumbled. He swore and then stared at it as if hypnotized. *That stupid chair!* It was the symbol of his betrayal. It mocked him; taunted him with the knowledge it had been purchased with the bet money Lynette had won on their wedding day.

I'll get even with you, you detestable chair! he raged. In a crazed fury he dragged the chair to the patio door and shoved it out onto the concrete. Panting, he rushed into the garage, rummaged wildly and at last found what he wanted. He ran back outside, threw the contents of the can over the chair and tossed a lighted match on top. The chair burst into a great, roaring inferno. Black smoke poured heavenward. He laughed hysterically as tears ran down his cheeks. In a matter of minutes the proud chair was reduced to a broken, blackened skeleton and a small pile of ashes. He kicked it for good measure, scattering the pieces across the patio. Then he turned and went inside.

The house was a sepulcher of silence. John looked blankly around him. He started across the room, for what purpose he knew not. Something crunched under his foot. It was the lollipop Todd had thrown as Lynette took him out the door. Hysteria rose again in choking sobs, making it impossible to breathe. He bent slowly and picked up the lollipop. It was so typical of Lynette; always bribing her way through to get what she wanted. But it was also the last thing Todd's small fingers had touched. The floodgates opened. He threw himself on the sofa. Great, wrenching sobs shook his body. He wept until all the bitterness and rage washed out of him, leaving him physically and emotionally exhausted, and he slept.

The persistent ringing of the telephone slowly brought him back to reality. He kept his eyes closed and did not move. He did not want to talk to anyone. The ringing finally stopped and he escaped again into sleep. He had no idea how long he slept this time, but it was again the ringing of the telephone that wakened him. He had a terrific headache. The nagging ring echoed inside his head. He would have to answer it to shut it up. He dragged himself to the phone and picked it up.

"John?"

"Yes," he mumbled through thick lips.

"This is Marlin," the voice said.

"Marlin," John repeated slowly and stupidly. He could not think. Why would Marlin be calling.

"Are you all right?" Marlin asked in alarm.

No. Go away and let me alone.

"Are you alone?" Marlin asked swiftly when there was no answer.

"Yes."

"Mom said Lynette was going to take Todd today. She is worried about you and tried to call earlier but nobody answered. You sound as if you shouldn't be alone. Is there anyone who could come and stay with you?"

"I don't want anybody," John said flatly.

"Would you care if I came?" Marlin asked gently. "Or Mom and Pop?"

"I guess not."

"We'll be there then," Marlin said as if it were already settled. "Just hold on until we get there."

John replaced the receiver of the telephone to its cradle. He was tired—so tired. He flopped on the sofa again and closed his eyes. He had come to the end. There was nothing left to live for and no reason to go on. The thought of suicide had entered his mind more than once before. He had always pushed it aside, knowing it would solve nothing and telling himself he had to live for Todd's sake. Now there was absolutely nothing left to live for. The idea of ending his misery in death enticed him more than ever before.

He wondered which would be the best way. He wanted to be sure he did it right. An unsuccessful attempt would be worse than not trying. His mind functioned very slowly, but he had plenty of time. He knew it would take several hours for Marlin to come. Somehow even that call seemed unreal now. He must have imagined it. No one was coming. No one would ever come. For the rest of his life he would be alone. He would just lie on the sofa until he starved to death. But if Marlin *was* coming, that would not work. He must do something that worked faster than starving.

Slowly, his irrational mind sorted over the alternatives again. The only sure way was to shoot himself, he decided at last. He sat up and then slowly made his way to the drawer where he kept his revolver. He moved slowly as if in a black dream, feeling unattached to himself. His fingers shook uncontrollably. He could scarcely load the revolver. Finally it was done. His knees buckled and he slumped to the floor. His head dropped on his chest and his hands hung between his knees, the revolver clutched tightly in his fingers. He heard and saw nothing but the hopelessness of the deep, black pit of depression into which he had fallen. He could see no way out.

Chapter 29

John drifted in and out of sleep as the morning light crept into the room. He was aware of soft footfalls and whispering voices in the next room. But, unwilling to face the day, he gave no sign of waking. He knew he had failed again. It seemed as though he had failed at everything he had ever tried to do. He had not even succeeded in taking his own life. Only dimly could he remember what had transpired the evening before. He had not heard anyone coming in. He knew only that someone had pried the revolver from his fingers. A doctor had materialized from somewhere and he was given an injection. Then there had been only the blackness of drugged sleep until now.

"Would you like a cup of coffee, John?" a tender voice beside him asked.

He opened his eyes slowly and struggled to sit up. The smell of the coffee and his ingrained courteousness compelled him to accept the cup his mother offered.

"How do you feel this morning?" Pop asked as John sipped slowly.

"Tired," he answered dully. He leaned back and closed his eyes. He knew he should be glad to have been rescued from death. But he did not know how he could face the ordeal of living another day. If he had only been sure that oblivion would come with the click of the revolver, he would not have hesitated a moment. But he had not been sure. Instead of oblivion, he might be face to face with God—a God he was not ready to meet. It was too painful to live any longer but he was afraid to die. There were no easy alternatives.

"The doctor said you should rest for a few days," Pop said. "He left some pills that will make you sleepy so you can rest. You are to take another one this morning."

John took and swallowed the pill that lay on his father's extended palm. He had no strength to protest. His mind was clear enough to remember the arrangements he had made to sell the house and its contents. Since then some of those plans were changed. But he lacked the strength to complete them. Pop and Mom suggested he move home for awhile instead of renting a place of his own.

Pop was busy filling silo at home. He could not remain in Allendale for more than one day. So it was decided he would return home, leaving Mom and Marlin to help complete the sale of John's property and bring him home. Docilely, John agreed to all their plans. He would have agreed to anything they suggested. He felt completely unqualified to make any choices. He was a total failure and ready to let someone else make the decisions for him.

During those final days in Allendale, he gradually became grateful for the presence and help of his mother and brother. Together they sorted through the possessions that had accumulated in nearly four years of marriage. He had already contracted with an auction firm to dispose of the contents of the house. The appliances had been included with the sale of the property. They had only to go through each room and pack the personal items and valuables he wanted to keep. The pile of things to take along was very small in comparison to what he was leaving behind.

The effects of the pills he took during those days made him lethargic and unfeeling as he saw his house torn apart and sold. He felt no remorse when the final settlement was made on the property. Neither was there any anticipation for the future when he thought of returning home. He lived only a moment at a time, dully taking whatever it brought to him.

Eventually, the house was stripped bare. The auction firm had emptied it of all its contents. John's things were loaded for the trip home. They stopped at the real estate office long enough to turn in the last house key, and then it was all over. There was nothing more to do but leave town.

Marlin took the wheel of John's car, and Mom joined him in the front at John's suggestion. He settled himself in the space they had left empty on the back seat. He leaned back and closed his eyes. He remembered the day he had first seen Allendale. It seemed as though since then he had been beating his way through the tangled underbrush in a thick forest. He had gone in a full circle without accomplishing anything. He was going back home now to the starting place, broken and empty. A section of his life, but more, a part of himself was being left behind. His whole being ached for the son that could not go with him. Tears stung his eyelids and slipped unheeded down his cheeks. His companions, sensing his reticence, wisely left him to himself. Emotionally exhausted and physically drained, he slept.

Back home, in his loneliness for Todd, John retreated inside the shell of his own mental world. He found himself observing the family as they moved about him as if he were watching them through a plate glass window. He felt detached from all that went on around him. Life followed the familiar pattern it had always taken. While details varied with the days and the seasons, the pattern had changed little in the last six years. Though in a way it seemed nothing had changed, yet everything had. And nothing would ever be the same again. It was Jim and Carl who helped Pop in the barn now rather than John and Marlin. Becky's brood had grown to three preschoolers. The twins were approaching adolescence. Marlin and Jane had resumed the courtship which had been interrupted by his years in British Honduras. Their wedding day was fast approaching now.

"Are you *sure* Jane is the one for you?" John asked gravely as Marlin prepared to leave for his date a week before the wedding. "Once you are married it's too late to change your mind."

Marlin returned the comb to its place and faced John. "I know what you mean," he nodded. "I guess the way things went for you has made me do a lot of serious thinking. That's why Jane and I didn't get married as soon as I got back. We decided to wait awhile and see if we still feel the same as we did before. Sometimes people change with time and experience. After being apart for so long, we felt we needed to get reacquainted."

"That's right," John approved. "Take your time. You have your whole life ahead of you. Don't spoil it by rushing into something that isn't right for you."

"Jane is a wonderful person and we love each other. But most of all we want the Lord's will. We wanted to give Him time to show us if it is not His will for us to spend our lives together."

"Just be sure. That's all I can say." John expelled a slow breath audibly. "Just be sure."

Gradually John recovered from his near collapse. The kindness shown to him shamed him. He grew restless with the inactivity and began to help with the farm work. It felt good to be working outdoors again and doing something constructive. Much as he would have liked to stay in the antiseptic environment of the home place, surrounded by the circle of his family's love, he knew he could not remain there forever. He felt more like a guest than a family member, as though he really belonged elsewhere. Guilt smote him whenever he lit a cigarette, knowing Pop and Mom disapproved. He wished he could quit, but he had no strength to battle against his nicotine addiction. He compromised by going outside to smoke, but that only increased his feeling of ostracism.

John lowered the newspaper and cleared his throat. He looked across the table spread with farm ledgers to his father. "I've been thinking," he began. "It's time I found a place of my own. I've been looking at what is available for rent around here."

Pop looked up quickly. "You are welcome to live here as long as you like. You haven't worn out your welcome yet," he grinned.

"I know," John admitted without returning the smile. "You have all been good to me—better than I deserve. And I appreciate it. But time changes things, and I don't really belong here anymore. I can't be a guest forever."

"It's up to you," Pop yielded. "But if you have your own place, you will have rent to pay."

"I've been checking the ads for a job, too,"

John said. "There are a couple of possibilities but nothing especially exciting. I can't be too picky though. I still have some debts to pay off."

"I met Enos Hostetter in town the other day," Pop said. "He heard you were back home and asked about you. He wondered if you'd be interested in working for him again. They are really busy right now and he could use an extra hand. Think you'd like to go back to carpentering again?"

"I might," John considered. "I have to work somewhere."

"Enos said to tell you to call him if you're interested." Pop picked up his pen and flipped the page in his ledger.

John folded the paper and stood up. It was almost too easy. He had a job if he just said the word. He had liked carpenter work before and supposed he may as well do it again. He did not have any other good ideas.

The amount of the rent was the biggest deciding factor in his choice of a place to live. He was pleased to find a furnished trailer on the east side of the small town near the home farm. It was not new but it was quite satisfactory. Moving in was simple and quickly accomplished. It was with some misgivings that his mother watched him leave. Though he assured her he could keep house for himself, somehow a man living alone seemed unnatural to her. Only when she extracted a promise from him to be a frequent guest at her table did she become resigned to his leaving.

John managed the housework suitably by himself. It was the awful loneliness, not the housework, that was the greatest problem. When Lynette had left him, he had still had Todd. When Todd had been taken away, the vacuum had been partially filled by the home folks. Now he had cut himself off from them. They were busy with their own lives, and he did not expect them to coddle him. The men he worked with were friendly, but there was no one to socialize with. He did not fit with the single men or the married. He was a misfit in society. The long, lonely evenings haunted him with the ghosts of the past.

He grew desperate to see Todd. The judge had given him visiting rights every other weekend and alternate holidays. So far, all his attempts to call Lynette to arrange a visit had been unsuccessful. Either the phone was not answered, or she was not in. He left a message several times, but his calls were not returned. At last he could wait no longer. He decided to go without making prior arrangements and take the chance of finding

Todd at home.

John drove slowly up the winding drive toward the imposing structure that, according to the Martinsburg address Lynette had given him, was now Todd's home. The elegance of the house and the professionally landscaped grounds testified all too well of the wealth of its owner. *If money is what she wants, she got it this time*, he thought bitterly.

He parked his car in the semicircle drive and mounted the steps of the columned portico. His heart hammered in his chest, and cold sweat broke out on his forehead as he pushed the bell. It was Lynette herself who opened the door.

"You!" she sputtered in disbelief. "What are you doing here?"

"I have come to see Todd," he said evenly. "I've been trying to make arrangements to visit him for the last six weeks. I got tired of trying so I just came."

"Well, you can't see him," she stated flatly.

"Why not?" He glared at her.

"Because—he isn't here," she finished quickly.

"You lie," he accused. "He's here. You don't *want* me to see him."

"It will just upset him if he sees you. Can't

you see it's much better if you just go away and forget about us?" she asked in a tone that implied he was a simpleton.

"You think I can forget my son just like that?" He snapped his fingers. "*You*, I would gladly forget. But Todd? Never! He's still my son. The judge gave me visiting rights. You can't keep me from seeing Todd," he cried in exasperation. "Either let me in or bring him here."

"I'm sorry, Mr. Shenk, but it is not possible. I told you he is not here. Now please go away. I'm very busy." Abruptly, she shut the door in his face.

Fool! John chided himself as he reached his car. *Did you really think she would let you see him? You knew why she didn't return your calls.*

He stood looking at the house, searching the windows in vain for the sight of a small face. Perhaps she was telling the truth this time. Maybe Todd was not home. Dejectedly he got back in the car and drove away. At the end of the winding drive he stopped. He had no plans. He did not feel like going home to his lonely trailer, and yet there was nothing to do here if he could not see Todd. He circled around towards Allendale. He would drive by the Eisleman home. It was a long chance, but he felt he could not go home without at least trying.

His heart skipped a beat when he neared the house and saw two forms on the lawn. Lynette's father was raking the last leaves of the barren trees. Beside him romped a small figure in sturdy coveralls that could be none other than Todd. Hastily, he parked at the curb and leaped out of the car.

"Todd! Todd!" he cried as he lunged towards the boy.

Todd turned and with a half-strangled cry ran towards John. "Daddy!" he squealed with delight, flinging himself into his father's arms. It was the long-desired reunion John had imagined so often and was all he could have hoped for. They were lost in the joy of each others' presence and oblivious to anything else around them.

"I knowed you'd come," Todd cried, patting John's cheek.

His emotions rendering him speechless, John merely squeezed the boy and kissed him again.

"And what is the meaning of this?" John felt a hand on his shoulder. He looked up, suddenly aware of Lynette's father's disapproval. "Does Lynette know you are here?"

"I just came from her place," he evaded the question.

"She told us not to let you see him," Mr.

Eisleman nodded towards Todd. "I had no idea you were in town."

"I have visiting rights every other weekend," John pointed out. "She can't deny me those rights. Now if you'll excuse us, we'll be going. I'll bring him back to you tomorrow evening, I assure you."

"But—" Mr. Eisleman started to protest, "you can't—"

But John and Todd were already getting in the car. John spun the wheel and dodged out into the traffic. He had Todd! It was almost too good to be true.

For two glorious days, John reveled in Todd's presence. The Shenks were delighted when John arrived with his precious cargo. Only then did he think of clothing. Todd had only what he was wearing. Becky's son, Chris, was nearly the same age, and she gladly loaned Todd what he needed.

Much too soon it was time to take Todd home again. The closer they got to Allendale, the lower John's spirits sank. He did not know how he could bear to part with Todd a second time. He handed Todd to his grandfather and abruptly turned to leave without going inside.

Mr. Eisleman left Todd in the house and stepped out the door. "You better not try this again," he said in a low voice. "Lynette

303

was furious when she found out what happened."

"I was within my legal rights," John defended himself.

"I know," Mr. Eisleman said. "I truly feel sorry for you, but it is better if you don't come back. I know that is hard to understand, but you are only making things more difficult for yourself and everyone else if you insist on seeing Todd. He cried himself to sleep for days and kept asking for you for a long time. He was afraid of Tom. Lynette thought he was finally getting adjusted now to his new life. It will take a long time to undo the damage you have done this weekend."

Damage? John thought angrily as he drove home. *How can I damage my son by visiting him for a weekend?*

Against his will, he finally had to admit to himself that what Mr. Eisleman had said was true. The empty trailer was more conspicuously empty since it had been graced briefly by the presence of a small boy. The loneliness was more poignant than ever. He could see Todd in pajamas eating cold cereal at his table, Todd snuggled beside him in bed, Todd asking questions and laughing as they played together. He almost wished now he had not brought the boy there.

Was he to have no happiness at all? Everything he touched turned to ashes under his fingers. The only measure of happiness he had ever known had been temporary. Had he ever known any true happiness? The kind that did not fade? Did such a thing even exist?

Chapter 30

Reaching up to the ledge above the door, John's fingers sought and found the spare key that was kept there. He unlocked the door and let himself into his parents' home. The aroma that greeted him in the kitchen promised good things to come. He readily accepted his mother's frequent invitations to Sunday dinner, knowing his culinary skills could never equal hers. But it was more than the food that drew him. The afternoon of companionship was just as inviting.

He had come early, though he knew the family would not be home from church yet. But now that he had come he did not know what to do while he waited. He paced restlessly around the living room, raised a shade, sat down, and got up again. He looked in the oven and checked on the kettles sitting on top of the stove. Everything was under control. Returning to the living room, he wondered if perhaps he should have accepted his father's invitation to join them at church. At least it would have been something to do. Which would be worse, to be stared at or to be alone?

In an effort to find something to occupy his mind, he fell to his knees in front of the bookcase, searching for something interesting to read. There were all sorts of books, from children's literature to doctrinal study books. He leafed idly through a few, but nothing held his attention.

He stood up and was about to turn away when he saw his father's study Bible lying on top of the bookcase. He had not noticed it before. Pop had looked up a verse at the last minute that morning for the Sunday school class he was teaching and had neglected to put the Bible away. It was open to the Book of Hosea. John glanced at it briefly. He had never read much of the Old Testament prophets. He would have lost interest now if the words in chapter two had not leaped out at him.

"And she shall follow after her lovers, but she shall not overtake them; and she shall seek them, but shall not find them: then shall she say, I will go and return to my first husband; for then was it better with me than

307

now" (Hosea 2:7).

John stared. *What's this? I never knew there was anything like this in the Bible. What is it all about?*

He picked up the Bible, sat down and began reading at the first chapter. He was so absorbed in what he was reading, he did not know anyone was home until he heard footsteps crossing the porch. Quickly, feeling foolishly guilty, he replaced the Bible, leaving it open as he had found it. But the words he had read did not vanish from his memory. Whenever he was not involved in the conversation, he found his mind returning to and wondering about the meaning of what he had read.

After returning to his trailer late that afternoon, he hunted his long-unused Bible. Eventually he found it and turned again to the Book of Hosea. He started reading again at the first chapter and read the entire book without stopping. The meaning of much that he read was not clear to him. But the message of Hosea's writing could not be misunderstood. The nation of Israel had been wayward in her relationship with God. Yet, in spite of the enormity of her sin, God still loved His people and yearned for them. He called them to repentance and promised restoration.

Turning back, he thoughtfully reread snatches from the book.

"For Israel slideth back as a backsliding heifer. . . . Ephraim is joined to idols . . . they have committed whoredom continually. . . . Ephraim is oppressed and broken in judgment. . . . For they have sown the wind, and they shall reap the whirlwind. . . . O Israel, thou hast gone a whoring from thy God. . . . Ye have plowed wickedness, ye have reaped iniquity; ye have eaten the fruit of lies: because thou didst trust in thy way. . . . Israel is an empty vine. . . . How shall I give thee up, Ephraim? how shall I deliver thee, Israel? . . . Mine heart is turned within me. . . . I will not execute the fierceness of mine anger, I will not return to destroy Ephraim: for I am God and not man. . . . O Israel, thou hast destroyed thyself; but in me is thine help. . . . O Israel, return unto the Lord thy God. . . . I will heal their backsliding, I will love them freely."

John leaned his head against the back of the sofa and closed his eyes. He was beginning to draw the parallels between himself and Israel. He was the backsliding heifer that refused to be led. He had committed spiritual whoredom. He was the one God was calling to return. But to answer that call would be to drive another wedge between

309

himself and Todd. It would decrease his already almost nonexistent chances of regaining his son.

Like a starving child who has found a source of nourishment, John's spiritual appetite had been aroused and demanded to be fed. He felt compelled to read the Word. The formerly long, lonely evenings were now too short as he spent them reading his long-neglected Bible. The old Book seemed completely new. He read now with a desire to know and understand what it said, not merely because it was expected of him. All he had heard through the years of teaching which he had taken for granted now came back to great advantage. He grasped quickly what one with less teaching would have puzzled over for weeks. The seed that had been sown years earlier and had lain dormant in his soul's winter, now sprouted as in the warmth of spring. It was all new, fresh, and strangely satisfying. Yet at the same time, it brought condemnation and conviction. A fierce battle raged in his soul.

Several times he considered going to church, but he always vetoed the idea. Fear of being made a public spectacle kept him away from his parents' church, and he was not inclined to try another one where he was a total stranger. But as his newly awakened spiritual sense grew, the importance of other people's opinions began to recede.

"It will probably be full at church tonight," Marlin remarked one Sunday afternoon. "Maybe you would like to come, John," he half asked, half invited. "A chorus is coming to sing."

"That sounds interesting," John admitted.

"Jane and I would be glad to take you with us," Marlin offered.

"No, thanks," John declined. "I'll go by myself."

Marlin knew what he was talking about, John decided, when he found the parking lot jammed. The church was packed. He had hoped to slip unnoticed into a back bench, but they were all filled. The usher, whom John remembered as a small boy, led him up to a vacant seat on the second bench from the front.

An expectant hush fell over the church as the chorus took their places on the risers. The wholesome looks of the singers impressed John. The girls, in their matching plain blue dresses, had a simple feminine beauty and dignity. The men, most of them young, exhibited unconsciously a strength of character in their clean-cut humble appearance.

The leader gave the signal, and the chorus

broke exuberantly into song. From the first note, John was intrigued with the harmony of the a cappella singing. He had been away from it for so long that he had forgotten how beautiful it was. Much time and effort had obviously gone into preparing for this program. But more than that, he sensed they sang from the heart. Their faith and sincerity was not a facade.

As the program progressed, John's attention began to focus more on the words they sang than on the singers. They spoke to him in a way no sermon could have done. Many of the songs seemed to be especially for him; they fitted his needs and circumstances so well. They sang of Jesus' love and forgiveness, of His great understanding and help in trouble. John's eyes burned and his throat tightened when a girls trio sang:

Like a child by the seashore building castles in the sand,
Foolish dreams I had dreamed day by day,
Leaving God out completely till the day my castles grand
Fell apart in the tide and swept away.

Castles built upon the sand though they seem to be so grand
Will surely melt away for in life's storms they cannot stand.

In the Rock of the Ages all my hopes are
    built today
And in that Rock they will never pass
    away.*

John's head dropped. This was the root of
his problem. It was not all Lynette's fault his
life was a mess. It was not his parents' fault,
or the minister's fault, or the church's fault,
and certainly not God's fault. It was his own
fault. He had never built firmly upon the
Rock. He had built on the sand, and now it
was all swept away by the tides of time. The
only thing he could do was to start over and
build on the Rock this time.

But will God take me? his broken heart
cried. *After I've turned my back on Him, He
has every right to turn His back on me. It
isn't fair to live as I have and then give the
wreck to God and expect Him to take it.*

"Return unto the Lord thy God," the
words of Hosea shouted. "Thou hast destroyed thyself, but in me is thine help. . . .
I will love. . . . I will heal."

The leader of the chorus turned to face the
audience. "We are going to sing the last song
tonight as an invitation," he said. "If you
have felt God speaking to you about anything
in your life that you know is not right, make

it right tonight as we sing this song. Answer the Lord's call in your heart. If you need help, make it known to someone after the service. Get rid of your burdens tonight and begin living in victory. Don't waste any more years in a life of sin."

The leader turned back to the chorus. John's heart hammered. His hands were clammy and cold. God was speaking to him. He had been speaking for a long time. He had spoken through Brother Gingrich's message years ago when John had first begun to backslide. God had spoken through John's parents, Sam's accident, and Sam himself when he had begun to recover. But John had not listened to any of the warnings. God had spoken more loudly as marital problems magnified, but John had not recognized His voice. It was only since he had lost Todd that he had begun to listen.

John looked at the chorus as they softly began to sing the last song. *I could be like those young men*, he thought. *Some of them are no older than I am. But I wasted all the opportunities and advantages I had. My life is ruined now. How foolish I have been!*

As if in agreement with his thoughts the chorus sang:

> Wasted years, wasted years, Oh how foolish,

As you walk on in darkness and fears;
Turn around; turn around; God is calling;
He's calling you from a life of wasted
years.*

John's resistance collapsed. He could struggle no longer. Completely oblivious to those
around him, he was aware only of the call of
God and his need. It was too compelling to be
ignored any longer. The tight little circle in
which he had imprisoned himself was encom-
passed by the circle of God's boundless love.
He could not, would not resist it. Peace with
God was all that mattered.

He buried his face in his hands. "Oh
God!" he groaned inwardly. "I've made such
a mess of my life. If it is worth anything to
You, take it and make it whatever You want.
Forgive me for Jesus' sake."

It was not, by any standards, a formal
prayer. It was the anguished cry of a sincere
heart, the plea God had been longing to
hear. Divine arms circled the prodigal and
restored him to his place as a son and heir of
the kingdom. In John's soul, peace replaced
anguish. Despair turned to joy as the assurance of God's forgiveness and acceptance
flooded him. It was a miracle.

* Words from the song, "Wasted Years" by Wally Fowler.

Chapter 31

The moment John answered God's call did not mark the end of his search; it was more like a beginning. Surrendering to Christ is never over in a moment. When any human being gives himself to Christ, it is the beginning of eternity. And it becomes a more meaningful reality every day with no end to its dimensions.

The initial peace and forgiveness John experienced when he surrendered to Christ did not erase his past. He was not an entirely remade person when he got up the next morning. He was still a divorced man. He still ached terribly for Todd. He was still in debt and enslaved by the nicotine habit he had acquired along the way. But there was one major difference. He had found a Friend he could turn to any time he needed help, a

Friend who understood all about temptation, rejection, and sorrow. He could stop worrying about his problems and start trusting Christ to help him through each difficulty.

It was impossible to hide the change in his life, nor did he want to. One of the first, most noticeable changes was the absence of the small package he always carried in his shirt pocket. He had wished he could quit smoking before, but now he was determined to do it. He decided the only way was to get rid of the tobacco. Acting immediately, he threw all his tobacco in the garbage. *That's the end of that!* he thought as he slammed the lid on the can.

It was the end of the tobacco, but not of his cravings for it. He found going without tobacco was much more difficult for him than giving up alcohol had been. He had never been addicted to alcohol, but his body cried out for nicotine. Bad habits fight to survive and die lingering deaths. But now, he was not fighting against his chains in his own strength. Every time the desire for nicotine surfaced, he could talk to his Friend who gave him the strength to overcome the desire. No one around him guessed the intensity of the battle that was fought and won within him.

Still, John was in no hurry to make a public confession. He wanted to study his Bible and come to a deliberate conclusion on his own personal beliefs. He had drifted along too long making his moves carelessly according to what suited his fancy at the moment. This time he would proceed cautiously. He would not unite with any congregation until he understood its teachings and believed them for himself.

Pop's well-stocked bookshelves contained everything from pamphlets and booklets to thick volumes and commentaries, all Biblically sound in content. He had acquired the library gradually over the years in his own quest for knowledge. All John needed was at his fingertips. He devoured truth with a zeal he had not known he could possess. He carefully studied the Eighteen Articles of Faith, painstakingly reading every reference cited. It took him much longer to study through Daniel Kauffman's *Doctrines of the Bible*. But the more he read and understood, the more he believed. In turn, the more he believed, the greater became his peace and joy. As peace and joy multiplied, anxiety and despair faded.

Before he finished *Doctrines of the Bible*, it became evident to everyone that a transformation was ensuing in his life. Like a butterfly emerging from its cocoon, he was emerging into the fullness of life. He learned to smile and laugh again. He was able to enjoy the simple things of life with a genuine pleasure he had thought was lost forever. For the first time in his life he actually looked forward eagerly to attending worship services, not for the social benefits, but for fellowship with his Lord.

A new, close relationship developed between John and Marlin, for he found his brother always ready to help in the learning and growing process. If he had not been compelled to work to pay his debts, he would have spent more time in Bible study. Yet, the hours he spent pounding nails and sawing lumber could also be used to meditate on the truths he was continually discovering.

The red Mustang he drove stuck out like a sore thumb on the church parking lot and embarrassed him. He traded it in on a VW without any regrets. It was actually a relief to be rid of it and break another tie with his old life.

He made several unsuccessful trips to visit Todd. The last time, a stranger answered when he knocked on the door of Tom and Lynette's house. The lady informed him that she and her husband had bought the house from the Leisawitzes. She was sorry, but she did not know where they had gone. Lynette's parents refused to give him the address. He tried to trace them through the phone company but no Thomas Leisawitz was listed in any of the exchanges he tried. They seemed to have vanished completely. The law required Lynette to inform John of any change of address, but the law could not be enforced until she was found. The only recourse was to hire a private detective.

Even this new blow could not disturb the joy of the Lord that now occupied the void in John's life. The bitter taste of his sorrows had a mellowing effect on his personality and gave him a depth of character that was entirely new.

Months of patient study and meditation nurtured his growing faith. As slowly as he had eased out of fellowship with the church, he now returned to its beliefs, teachings, and fellowship. The fear that he would be the object of stares and whispers in the presence of his earlier acquaintances proved to be unfounded. While some treated him a bit awkwardly at first, the overwhelming response was one of compassion and concern. The men and women alike welcomed his presence among them. He knew now they had never ceased to care for him even though they had not expressed their feelings to him before. Slowly he came to feel he belonged among them again. They were still his people, after all.

For nearly a year, John studied and grew in his faith. The most difficult struggle for him lay in coming to a final conclusion on the question of divorce and remarriage. He knew, without asking, the position his parents and their church held on the issue. If he chose to join their fellowship, remarriage for him was unquestionably prohibited as long as Lynette lived. Somehow, that seemed to be too heavy a cross for him to carry for life. He read extensively on the subject. Much of what he read agreed wholly or in part with what Reverend Lind told him after Lynette filed for divorce. There were many churches who accepted divorced and remarried people into their membership. Sometimes he felt like going to one of them and ending the debate that continually churned in his mind. But he knew mere church membership would not completely bring him peace so long as his own mind had not settled the question.

Many of the books he read gave convincing explanations that sounded reasonable and scholarly. Yet, when he had begun to study, he had determined to judge all he read by the unchangeable Word of God. At the end of each round of the silent debate that clamored in his thinking, he always found himself face to face with the plain, irrefutable statements of Romans 7:2, 3. "For the woman which hath an husband is bound by the law to her husband so long as he liveth; but if the husband be dead, she is loosed from the law of her husband. So then if, while her husband liveth, she be married to another man, she shall be called an adulteress: but if her husband be dead, she is free from that law; so that she is no adulteress, though she be married to another man." Marriage is permanent until death dissolves the union. No exceptions, no excuses.

The passage was a brick wall that could not be surmounted or slipped through. He believed the whole Bible was the infallible Word of God. He could not accept one part and reject another. It was either all truth or no truth. Ultimately, the question was not, "What does the Bible say?" but, "Do I believe what the Bible says?" When the answer to the second question was settled in his mind, the answer to the first one created no more problems. If he wanted to live at peace with God and himself, he must surrender his will completely to his Master, even if it meant living a celibate life. The battle was not easily won, but with the surrender came a sweet peace and joy that more than compensated for what was withheld.

When the date for fall communion approached, John was at last ready to be one with the church in belief and practice. He made an appointment with the bishop to see what could be done about being received back into fellowship.

"I feel responsible for the trouble you have gotten into," the bishop confessed when John had explained the nature of his call. "Somehow I was so busy I never took time to visit and counsel with you even when I knew you were backsliding. I was busy here, and you were in Allendale. I just never got around to doing what I wanted to. No matter how worthwhile my work may be, if I am too busy to try to reach a soul in trouble, I am too busy. I confess my error to you and to God. I need His forgiveness as much as anyone."

"There was a time when I blamed the church leaders for my condition," John acknowledged. "There should have been more supervision of the IWs by the church. But not every one lost out spiritually as I did. I could have maintained Christian fellowship if I had wanted to. I always slid along doing what came most easily. When others my age became Christians, so did I. At least I was baptized and joined the church. But I was never deeply rooted in my faith. When my friends in IW did questionable things, I did too. I chose my course myself."

"I'm sure God has forgiven you, and we can do no less," the bishop assured him. "You understand, of course, that you cannot remarry as long as your wife is still living. The Bible is clear on that. We will give the hand of fellowship to a divorced person, but only if they are not and do not remarry."

"I understand," John's voice was clear. "I not only accept the responsibility for my choices, I also accept the consequences. I intend to live a single life."

"Then I see no reason why we could not receive you back into fellowship this fall," the bishop said. "We will ask you to make a public confession. I think we could arrange to do that in conjunction with our preparatory service next month. You would be eligible then to participate in the communion service the following Sunday."

"I look forward to it." John agreed with the bishop's plans.

John's public confession in the church was the cause of much rejoicing among his own family as well as the congregation. After the formalities, he was given the opportunity to give his testimony.

"I have never given a public testimony before," John said as he faced the audience. "I feel terribly incapable of expressing my gratitude to God for His mercy. Isaiah 38:17 describes what the Lord has done for me. 'Behold, for peace I had great bitterness: but thou hast in love to my soul delivered it from the pit of corruption: for thou hast cast all my sins behind thy back.' I turned my back on God. He had every right to turn His back on me. Instead of that, He has turned His back on my sins—not me. Hymn number 343 expresses my feelings better than any of my own words could do. If the chorister will lead it, I will let it speak for me."

Pages rustled as John sat down. The voices of the congregation blended to sing:

> People of the living God, I have sought the world around;
> Paths of sin and sorrow trod, Peace and comfort nowhere found:
> Now to you my spirit turns,—Turns a fugitive unblest;
> Brethren, where your altar burns, Oh, receive me into rest.
>
> Tell me not of gain and loss, Ease, enjoyment, pomp, and power;

Welcome poverty and cross, Shame,
  reproach, affliction's hour.
"Follow me"—I know Thy voice; Jesus,
  Lord, Thy steps I see;
Now I take Thy yoke by choice, Light
  Thy burden now to me.

Few eyes were dry when the song ended.
Mom's throat had closed with emotion on
the first line, and Pop blew his nose shame-
lessly. They were tears, not of sorrow, but of
rejoicing.

At the close of the service, John found
himself thronged by well-wishers who
heaped upon him verbal encouragement and
God's blessings. Never had he felt so totally
encircled by love and forgiveness as at that
moment.

"I'm so glad for you," Becky murmured as
she and Ken greeted John together. "We've
been praying for this day for a long time."

"This is a new beginning for you," Ken
added. "I believe God can use you in a
special way for His glory."

"I can't imagine how," John said.

"Just wait on Him. He'll show you His will
in His time," Ken said with conviction.

Chapter 32

For several years, John's life followed a subdued pattern. Slowly he paid off his debts. He moved in a small circle with no great ambitions for the future. His spiritual and emotional life fluctuated, going up and down by turns. The first year was the most difficult. Every holiday and anniversary reopened painful wounds. He knew his own sin was the cause of his situation. God had forgiven him, but he found it more difficult to forgive himself than to accept God's forgiveness.

As he looked back now, he could see part of the reason for the failure of his marriage was his own. While it was true Lynette had tricked him into marriage, she never could have done it if he had not first sinned. She had cleverly laid a trap for him, and like an ox on its way to the butcher, he had walked into it. Her soft words, gentle touch, and open admiration were a subtle plot laid to make him vulnerable to her ultimate enticement. The highway of life is littered with the human wreckage of countless other men who have succumbed to the seduction of a flattering woman. The knowledge that he was not the first or last to fall did nothing to ease the pain of the fateful choice or to change its consequences. What had seemed so right at the moment then, now filled him with shame.

After their marriage, he had failed to meet Lynette's emotional needs. He recalled her proposal of a second honeymoon and her complaints that he never talked to her. Those were her attempts to reach out to him and try to revive their faltering marriage. He fantasized about what might have been if he had responded differently to various events in their marriage. But it was too late to change anything now. Things were the way they were and nothing could ever change it.

He had to admit that his marriage had failed because it lacked a solid foundation. He had not built upon the solid Rock, Jesus Christ. How tragically his failure confirmed the Scripture, "Except the LORD build the house, they labor in vain that build it."

Though he never forgot the past, he learned not to dwell upon it. The possibility that Lynette would return to him and join him in his faith was so remote it was too much to hope for. Yet, he knew with God nothing is impossible. He committed the situation to God, asking only that His will, whatever it was, be done. As he travelled through several years and nothing changed about the situation, he began to wonder if God had not heard or was refusing to answer. Then God showed John that just because nothing had changed did not mean He was not working. Whenever doubts arose, John reminded himself that he had already committed everything to a sovereign God. Then he could rest, trusting God to do what was best, even though he himself had no idea what God's best was.

The struggle to forgive himself, and Lynette as well, was the most difficult battle of his spiritual warfare. He hated himself, Lynette, and Tom by turns. Feelings of hatred for Lynette and Tom were accompanied by guilt. As a Christian he knew he was supposed to love his enemies, but in this situation it seemed impossible. Tom and Lynette's marriage was a continual state of adultery. He could not give them God's blessing nor could he honestly wish them happiness together.

"You can't love or forgive them," God answered the questions of John's anguished heart. "But I can. You are in Me. Let Me give you My love and forgiveness."

Forgiveness came slowly. It was not over the first time it was done. Every time feelings of rejection, hate, and bitterness surfaced, John had to forgive anew. It was the only thing, he learned, that would take away the hurt and bring release. He was often discouraged when he thought he had forgiven only to find the next day he needed to forgive again. Then he berated himself for not living victoriously, until God showed him that a victorious life was not one without battles, but one that continued on with God in spite of them. He learned to accept days of discouragement as normal and steps to the ultimate victory at the end of life.

As time went by and his spiritual growth continued, John began to realize God was using his situation to draw him to Himself. If the divorce had not occurred, he possibly would never have been in fellowship with the Lord. This knowledge helped him finally to accept the situation. Though God could not erase the past, He could give the ability to live above the situation and thus find deliverance. His growth was slow and often painful, but as his dependence on God grew, a Christlike character developed. He no longer needed the tutoring Marlin had given him in his faith's infancy. When Marlin and Jane moved to Georgia in answer to a call for workers in a mission outreach, John naturally missed his brother's companionship, but he was not bereft. He had learned to walk with the Lord alone.

The pace of his growth quickened when he accepted the responsibility of teaching a Sunday school class of intermediate boys. At first he was reluctant to accept, feeling they should have a teacher who had lived a more exemplary life. But the superintendent pointed out that lessons learned from past mistakes could actually add depth to his teaching. His personal testimony of the consequences of one small wrong choice and what it leads to could serve as a clear warning to boys who were hearing the Spirit's voice for the first time.

After thinking about it for a week, John decided to accept the call of the Lord through the church. In studying to teach this class, he uncovered many of the truths he needed to know for his own spiritual growth. It also gave purpose to his life and a sense of accomplishment. Not weighed down with the responsibilities of a family, he had more time to give to "his boys," as he called them. He frequently arranged ball games, rafting excursions, and hikes with them. He enjoyed the recreation as much as they did and found it made them more attentive in class. He was more than a teacher to be listened to for half an hour once a week; he was a personal friend. The relationship that developed between them was satisfying to everyone and helped to partially fill the void in his life, for like anyone else, he needed to feel useful and wanted by other people.

After several years, John began to feel he had reached a sort of plateau. He had come through the initial stages of his spiritual struggles, and though he still experienced some ups and downs, the downs were now only small dips rather than deep valleys. He was surprised to find he could go for days and weeks at a time without thinking of the problems that once nearly drove him out of his mind. He had thought then it would be impossible to live another hour. If someone had told him the time would come when he could go for many days without thinking about the situation, he never would have believed it. But now he was too busy and happy to dwell upon the past. He still thought of Todd often and wondered about him. It always brought a pang to his heart when he saw a two or three year old (for in his mind Todd never got any older than when he had last seen him), but he no longer ached with misery at the memory. At times it almost seemed like a dream that he had ever had a wife and son.

A strange restlessness he could not define began to take possession of him. The sense of fulfillment he had once found in teaching "his boys" somehow did not seem as satisfying as before. He spoke to no one of his feelings and even asked himself what was wrong. He wanted something more, but did not know what it was. He felt an indistinct call to some kind of Christian service, but unable to discover it, he let the matter rest with the Lord. Two more years passed as he waited and prayed, asking God to reveal His will for his life.

After a long, hot day of nailing shingles on a roof, it was good to go home and relax. John picked up his mail, leafing through it as he walked towards his trailer. Besides the electric bill there was only one other piece of mail that was of any value—a letter from Marlin. The brothers corresponded occasionally, though the majority of the news John read from Georgia came through the letters his mother received and shared with him.

Unlocking his door and letting himself in, John dropped onto the sofa and propped up his feet as he unfolded the letter and began to read. After the brief opening remarks, Marlin wrote:

I have decided to accept the position of program director that has been offered to me in the Wilderness Camp School in New Hope. Jane and I have prayed much about this before coming to a decision. We feel the Lord led us to Georgia but that it has been a station along the way to this work. We will be moving to Alabama in August in order to begin working there in early September.

I wonder if you have ever considered going into some type of service. The more I have seen of this school, the more I think it would be an ideal place for you. There is always a need for counsellors. Let me know if you are interested at all.

The letter concluded with bits of news about Jane and the two children. When he had finished, John went back and reread the two paragraphs about the move Marlin would be making. Marlin had written often about the Wilderness Camp School since the work had been started two years ago. He had always been excited about the work and helped frequently with special projects. The board of trustees felt now he could provide the kind of leadership needed to develop and improve the program.

From the beginning, John had been interested in the reports Marlin wrote of the school, though he had not become actively involved. He knew the school was for emotionally disturbed boys. The concept of a wilderness school was not entirely new, but this one was unique in that Christian principles were incorporated into the program, providing both emotional and spiritual healing. He had never told anyone about his undefined call to service. Was the Lord calling now through his own brother? He could not truthfully say he had never considered serving in another capacity than the one in which he was now involved. What he knew of the New Hope School did appeal to him. A new excitement stirred within him as he dropped to his knees to lay the matter before the Lord.

John answered Marlin's letter presently, saying he was interested in the work but would like to see it first. Marlin urged him to come. Accordingly, he arranged to take a week of vacation for that purpose and in late September arrived at the little town of New

Hope, Alabama.

Following Marlin's directions, he found the camp school situated in a forested area several miles from the town. The rustic construction of the main buildings blended well with the woodsy atmosphere and wilderness lifestyle of the school. He could easily see why Marlin had said the wilderness setting had a therapeutic effect on emotionally disturbed boys. The straightness and fragrance of the pine trees, chirping of birds, sparkling water of the lake, and expanse of blue sky overhead all blended to create a peaceful, quiet atmosphere.

Marlin had been looking for John and came out of the office building to greet him as he stepped out of his VW.

"So, you made it!" Marlin exclaimed, pumping his brother's arm. "Good to see you. How was the trip?"

The brothers chatted briefly, and then Marlin led the way inside the office building to Moses Miller's office. He introduced the two men and then left to return to his own desk. "I'll see you later," he called over his shoulder.

"Have a seat," Mr. Miller invited, waving to a chair opposite his desk. "Glad to have you here today."

"I'm glad to be here," John replied, grinning. "After two days in a VW, it's good to be able to stretch a little."

"I'm sure it is," Mr. Miller laughed. "Marlin tells me you are interested in knowing more about our school. I don't know what all he has told you, so you'll have to excuse me if I repeat some things you already know."

"New Hope Wilderness Camp School is a year-round residential camping program for boys between the ages of 10 and 18 who have emotional problems," Mr. Miller began in his soft-spoken way. "These boys are referred to us, often by the state, courts, or case workers, but sometimes privately by their parents. We are not an institution for the mentally retarded or drug addicts and that type of problem. Most of our boys come from broken homes and as a result have been emotionally damaged to the point they are unable to function normally in society. We isolate these boys from normal society and put them into a wilderness setting. The boys are normally enrolled in the program for one year although sometimes they stay a little longer.

"Our objectives include showing the boy his worth as an individual and returning him to society as a better functioning person. These boys have learned to consider themselves as failures. Quite often they have failed to find the love and acceptance they need as small children, and this has hampered their development in other areas. They have failed academically as well as socially. Camping is attractive and fun for boys of this age. We teach them to take personal responsibility for themselves, to learn to solve their problems, to understand themselves and others, to experience academic success, to learn good habits of personal hygiene, to learn how to be good citizens, and to use their talents creatively. All these principles are taught from a Christian perspective. We want not only to return boys to society who are able to function normally, but we want them to be Christian young men. Without Christ, they can never be totally emotionally healed.

"At present, we have thirty boys at New Hope," Mr. Miller continued, leaning back in his chair. "They are divided into groups of ten with two leaders to each group. We have many more applicants, but we are not able to accept more. There are two reasons for this: lack of finances and lack of personnel. If we add another group of ten, we will need two more group leaders. Unfortunately, it is more difficult to obtain group leaders than to find ten boys who need help. As the divorce rate increases, so does the number of emotionally damaged children.

"Being a group leader is not a small job. A group leader is a surrogate parent to the boys in his group. Counsellors must, of course, be male, in good health, emotionally and spiritually mature, single, and able to commit themselves for at least 18-24 months. Would you be able to make that kind of commitment?"

"Yes, I could," John nodded. "I don't know how much Marlin has told you of my personal life, but I am single and free from any other obligations."

"Marlin did tell me a little about your past," Mr. Miller admitted. "He said you were married and had a son, but your wife divorced you and took the boy. Do you ever get to see him?"

"No," John shook his head. "She disappeared and I haven't been able to trace him. He is eleven years old now. He may also be emotionally damaged because of our broken home. I don't know where he is and can't help him. But perhaps I can help other boys who have been hurt."

"You know, I always felt I could identify somewhat with these boys since my mother died when I was small and I was raised in a foster home," Mr. Miller said. "But you would be better able to identify with them than I. You have experienced rejection and know just how they feel. I think you would be well-suited to be a group leader in our program."

"I want to be sure it is the Lord's will before I attempt to join your work," John said. "I'll be staying with Marlin and Jane for three days. I'd like to watch the program in action, if it's all right with you, before I make a decision."

"Certainly," Mr. Miller agreed. "I do hope you decide to join us. We could certainly use your help."

John accompanied Marlin the next few days as he went about his work. The more he saw, the more convinced he became that this was the place the Lord wanted him to be.

"Well, what do you think by now?" Marlin asked the last evening of John's visit as Jane was putting the children to bed. "Think you'd like to come to stay?"

"Yes, I do," John answered. "I really feel this is where the Lord wants me. I wish I had gotten into something like this instead of going to Allendale. My life would undoubtedly be much different now."

"You know, our work here is to help troubled boys, but there is also another less noticeable objective," Marlin said seriously. "Since the draft has been abolished and our young men are no longer forced into service, very few of them volunteer. If our country became involved in another war, we have no promise what the government's position would be regarding conscientious objectors. And the church is not doing enough to prepare for that possibility. If we wait until we are forced to do something, we won't be able to create good programs like this fast enough to meet the need. We must have units functioning now so there are places in operation when they are needed. Besides helping troubled boys, we are also providing a place for our young men to spend some time in service."

"I've thought about that myself," John admitted thoughtfully. "For some, the Vietnam War is no more than a bad memory today. But soon a generation will be growing up that knows nothing about the draft. If they were put in a position like I was, would they be any better prepared to come through successfully than I was? The IW program was too loosely structured. We need to provide something better, that's true. But I think the core of the problem goes deeper. You said yourself you have trouble getting enough counsellors. Why is that?"

"The same reason it has always been, I suppose," Marlin said. "People are too materialistic and lack the vision of the work to be done."

"Exactly," John agreed. "If I hadn't been drafted, I probably would never have left my home community. Because there is no longer a draft and young men aren't forced into service, they rarely go. The church can't establish operating facilities without people willing to serve. So the problem boils down to personal commitment."

"You have a point there," Marlin agreed. "But if there are no programs calling for help, how will the people see the need? We need to provide both the call to service and the facilities for it."

"You're right," John acknowledged. "And I want to help every way I can."

Chapter 33

Arrangements for John's move to New Hope Wilderness Camp School progressed rapidly. Within a few weeks he found himself on the interstate, heading south again towards Alabama.

The first few months in camp were a training period. John learned to know the administrators and other staff members. A schedule of conferences and activities was arranged to give him on-the-job and in-service training. This time of preparation was vital to becoming a successful group leader. The more he learned about the problems of emotionally disturbed boys and the situations he would face as a group leader to them, the less qualified he felt to help them. But at the same time, the knowledge of the hurts and needs of these boys fed his growing desire to do what he could for them.

"You have done very well in your training period," Moses Miller told John in a private conference late one afternoon. "We feel you are ready to assume the responsibility of being a group leader now on your own."

John looked across the desk into the face of the middle-aged administrator he had come to appreciate in the short time he had known him. "Whatever you say," he assented.

"You are probably aware that Lynn Showalter's term expires this week. He is going back home to be married. You will be assigned to your first specific group of boys next week. You will be working with Joel Hege. He has been here for a year. I'm sure he will be able to help you with any unfamiliar problems or situations."

The ten boys in John and Joel's group were typical of all the other groups in the school. There were some whose behavior was violent and aggressive; others were withdrawn and silent. There was one perpetual comedian as well. It took much wisdom and patience to know how to handle each individual and the variety of situations. The number of boys in the group remained the same, though individuals frequently changed as some moved on to the next level of the program and new ones joined the group.

After six months at New Hope had passed, John had adjusted to the daily routine and was finding satisfaction in his work. It was thrilling to see a new boy join the group and help him experience emotional healing and achieve personal stability as he passed through the stages of the program. The outdoor life was appealing to the boys, and John enjoyed the hikes, fishing trips, campfire talks, cookouts, and campsite maintenance work as much as his charges.

Being a group leader meant being just that—a leader. As much as possible, John led the group in learning to work together, to interact companionably, and to settle their differences among themselves. This was accomplished better by gently leading than by forcibly driving. He was on duty five 24-hour-days a week. This plan was more beneficial than an eight-hour workday. In this way the boys could not play one group leader against another, nor could group leaders put off solving problems until the next group leader arrived to relieve them. Living with and sharing the environment of the boys made working together and solving problems a continuing process. But group leaders also needed some time to themselves to maintain their own stability. The two days off after five

days on duty was a necessary and refreshing break.

The Sundays when John was on duty, he
attended the chapel on the camp grounds
with his group of boys. When he was off
duty, he attended the small Mennonite
church in town. Most of the people in the
congregation were connected in some way
with the camp school, but there were also a
few families in the area who attended as
well. Because of the boys' immaturity and
lack of teaching, the chapel services at camp
were kept on an elementary level. It was
stimulating for John to attend services in the
church where the deeper things of the Word
were taught.

"Excuse me," John apologized as he
opened the church door one Sunday to step
out and nearly ran into a young lady who was
just about to come in. He stepped aside and
held the door open for her to pass through.
"You're new around here, aren't you?" he
asked politely. "Are you with the school?"

"Yes," she smiled, offering her hand in
greeting. "I came last week. I'm helping in
the kitchen."

John shook the proffered hand. "I'm a
group leader at the school. John Shenk is my
name. And yours?"

"Sylvia Detweiler."

346

"Glad to meet you," John returned her smile. "Welcome aboard. I don't see much of the cooks, but I enjoy the meals they make for us."

"Thank you," Sylvia said as she turned to go on. "I'll see you around."

That first brief conversation between John and Sylvia was entirely by accident and simply a friendly introduction. But as time elapsed, John became uneasy about their relationship. He did not seek to develop anything more than a casual acquaintance with her. Nor did she go out of her way to meet him. But whenever their paths crossed, she always had a smile and some friendly words for him. Without forethought he found himself looking for her when he took his group into the dining hall. At night, after lights out, he could picture her face and the soft smile that lighted her features. She was not exquisitely beautiful, but she was lovely in her own way. Her soft-spoken, gentle ways were the only ornaments she needed to make her attractive. In her upper twenties, she was only a little younger than himself.

Stop it! he commanded himself. *Don't think such things. You were married and don't forget it.*

It was strange, when he thought about it,

that he had to remind himself he had once been married. It seemed a long time ago, and almost as though it had happened to someone else. His life now was so completely different.

There's nothing to make me think Sylvia thinks of me as anything more than a friend, he told himself. *I dare not let myself think of her as more than a casual friend or give her any reason to think she is more than that to me. I wonder if she knows I was married.*

From then on John made an effort to keep his mind and eyes from wandering in Sylvia's direction. He was still friendly if he chanced to meet her, but there was a reserve in his manner that had not been there before. She noticed the change and did not understand it. His reserve and her puzzlement erected a barrier between them neither knew how to surmount. She could not ask him what had come between them without giving him the impression their friendship had ever meant anything special to her. Nor could he explain his marital status to her without implying he thought she was interested in him as more than a friend when he was not even sure that was the case. The situation was stalemated.

Slylvia's hands flew as she dried and stacked the plates. They froze suddenly when she heard Edward Eby and his wife, who also worked in the kitchen, speaking of John.

"I know he feels the Lord is using it for good," Mrs. Eby said, "but I can't help feeling sorry for him anyway. He's never heard anything of his son, has he?"

Sylvia turned her back to hide the sudden trembling of her hands. *Son?!*

"No. His wife just disappeared with the boy and they were never heard from or found since," Edward answered. "He says losing the boy on top of the divorce nearly drove him to suicide. You'd never think he would have been like that; he's so different now."

"He has a wonderful testimony," Mrs. Eby agreed, "but how much better it would have been if he had never slipped away from the Lord."

Sylvia's mind whirled. The pieces of the puzzle suddenly fell into place. John's sudden reserve was not because of anything she had done. He could not cultivate a relationship with any woman so long as his former wife lived. He could never be more than a casual friend to her or any other woman. The possibility that he was not a bachelor had never entered her mind. She had just assumed he had always been single. Though her appreciation for him did not

349

lessen, yet what she had learned changed her attitude toward him.

John never knew how or when Sylvia learned of his marital status, for no words of explanation ever passed between them. Yet he was sure she must have learned of it sometime. She was as friendly and polite as before, but with the same discretion as to any of the other married men.

The old hurts, that John had thought he was through battling, resurfaced. He fantasized about what might have been if he had never married Lynette. The thought of a happy home with a sweet Christian wife and children of his own was as appealing to him as to any other healthy man. He wept for a love that could never be. Once again he struggled through feelings of anger and bitterness toward forgiveness and victory. It did not come easily. All the pat answers that come so glibly from the lips of those who had never shared a similar experience could not automatically take away the loneliness he felt. Those around him were not aware of the fierce battle that raged in his heart. He fought it solitarily.

Off duty and alone in his bedroom, John's soul was torn in agony. He knelt by his bed, pouring out his loneliness and frustration to the only One in whom he could confide the inmost longings of his humanity. As he prayed, the words of the psalmist spoke softly to his heart. "The Lord is my Shepherd, I shall not want."

"What do you mean, Lord?" John asked. "I know you are taking care of me. You supply my needs."

"I am all you need, but not all you want. My child, I can be all you want."

John hesitated. "I can't honestly say I'm willing right now, Lord," he cried at last. "But I'm willing to be made willing. Let me be satisfied with You alone. The Lord is my Shepherd, I shall not want anything else."

With that, John felt an overwhelming nearness of a divine Presence. This was followed by a peace he had never known before. It filled him with a reverential awe. Then a great bursting of joy flooded his heart, washing away all desire for anything more. The tempest in his heart was stilled, and there was a great calm. He was satisfied and secure within the circle of God's great love.

Chapter 34

The memory of his total submission to God's will and the subsequent sense of God's Presence and peace gave John a new determination to accept life as it was and not wallow in regrets for the mistakes of the past. With a renewed zeal, he threw himself heart and soul into his work.

David Hinton came into John's group of boys soon after this experience of surrender. In working with this extremely aggressive boy, John needed the assurance of God's presence more than at any time since he had come to New Hope. A neglected and abused child, David had been abandoned by his natural mother soon after birth. He had been beaten by his father when he was three years old. The head injury sustained in the beating caused permanent damage to his inner ear, leaving him hard of hearing. Speech therapy had been needed to help him learn to pronounce words clearly. Because of the neglect and abuse of his father and stepmother, David had been placed in the custody of the state. His father was currently in prison on a burglary charge. His stepmother had no interest in him.

David had lived in twenty different foster homes and institutions in the last eight of his fourteen years. All the foster home placements were unsuccessful because of his violent temper and aggressive outbursts. He had been in trouble with the law for various offenses, most of them involving the theft of firearms, which seemed to especially fascinate him.

David described himself as a loner. He deliberately avoided close contact with others because he had never experienced any lasting relationships. He had learned that developing an attachment to anyone only resulted in pain when he had to move on to another home or institution. To him, New Hope was simply another institution to be endured. He maintained an aloof and scornful attitude toward John and the other boys in the group. He lived for the day when he would be old enough to be allowed to leave school and support himself. He was sure when he was on his own he would not have to take orders from anyone, and then things would be much better.

Even though David was failing in school, he insisted he did not care. He felt he was so far behind he would never catch up anyway. He thought people regarded him as a "crazy dunce." He was especially sensitive to teasing. He often imagined unintended threats in the remarks of others and reacted with impulsive anger. Without thinking, he would strike out and hit someone or destroy property. It tried John's patience to the limit when there was still another bloody nose or broken tool to deal with after they had gone through the same type of problem over and over again. They seemed to have made so little progress in the battle against David's violent temper. There could be no progress until David accepted the responsibility for his actions. But he always blamed other people or circumstances for what he did wrong, claiming he was unable to control his temper and nothing could be done about it.

John was sure the tough, scornful appearance David maintained was only a veneer to the neglected, unwanted, and bewildered person within. If he could only find the crack in David's veneer he would have the key to unlock the secrets of the real David.

Fishing trips were a favorite activity with John's group. Just as they were preparing to return from one such excursion they ran into difficulty.

"What's the matter with this thing?" John asked in dismay after he had pulled the rope of the outboard motor for the sixth time and it still refused to start. Various suggestions were offered and tried to no avail. He looked up at the threatening clouds overhead. "If we have to walk back around the lake we'll be soaked to the skin from the looks of those clouds," he remarked. "David, do you have any idea what could be wrong with this motor?" he asked, glancing over to the boy who stood aloof from the group as usual.

David casually sauntered over and squatted down beside the motor. Wordlessly, he tinkered with it a few moments and then looked up. "If I had a Phillips screwdriver I could fix it," he said.

John reached under the seat, drew out a small tool set and opened it. "Will this do?" he asked, withdrawing a small tool.

"I think so," David nodded. He bent over the motor, working intently, absorbed in what he was doing. The group gathered around, watching. After a few minutes, David stood up. "Now try 'er," he said, wiping his hands on his pants.

John pulled the rope twice and the motor sputtered to life. The boys cheered and slapped David on the back.

"Aw, that was nothin'," David acted embarrassed. But John knew he was pleased by the grin that spread across his face. "I used to fool with engines all the time in the shop at the one place I lived."

The motor purred smoothly all the way back across the lake. They were nearly to the dining hall when the first drops of rain began to fall. David was the hero of the day. Several boys mentioned it during the campfire talk that evening. John saw the hunger for acceptance in David's eyes and reinforced their praise, driving a wedge into the crack of his carefully guarded veneer. The key John had been seeking had been given to him in an unexpected time and place, on something as ordinary as a fishing trip.

The change in David's attitude was so subtle at first it was nearly imperceptible. But like anyone else, he had a deep need to be accepted and useful. John had discovered David's natural mechanical aptitude and capitalized on that talent now whenever possible. Being able to accept the rewards of honestly deserved praise was the first step in achieving self-acceptance.

David's progress was slow and not steadily

upward. Sometimes it seemed he took two steps backward for each step forward. Since the group worked together, David's setbacks affected and frustrated the whole group. It was not easy for the group to withhold judgment when David's lack of cooperation caused them to miss a meal or activity. But slowly, with the help of John and his group, he learned to accept personal responsibility for his actions and solve his problems.

As David's emotional stability improved, his interest in spiritual things began to grow. At first he had scorned any religious activity, enduring it only because it was required. Though he did not become an enthusiastic participant now, he did listen attentively during chapel.

David enjoyed a ball game as much as any of the boys. When he played, he played to win and not merely for the exercise. The game was in full swing one evening when he stepped up to bat. He connected with the ball on the second pitch and sent the ball far afield. He rounded the bases swiftly and though it meant taking a chance, raced for third. He saw the ball coming towards the third baseman and slid in to the base in a cloud of dust.

"Out!" the umpire called as David was tagged.

"I am not out!" David disagreed, jumping up and facing the umpire.

"Sorry," the umpire said, beginning to turn away.

But David could not so easily accept the umpire's decision. "You're crazy!" he yelled, turning livid with rage. He ranted and raved, calling the umpire all sorts of descriptive names. John tried to calm David, but without success. "Play your crummy game without me," David cried angrily. "Anybody with half an eye could see I was safe. If you guys won't play fair, I'm not going to help."

He stalked off the ball diamond and plopped on the ground. He would sit and let them play without him. He didn't have to help.

"All right, David," John shrugged. "Sit until you are ready to cooperate."

Left alone, David's impulsive anger cooled. He knew he had been unreasonable. He had not really wanted to drop out of the game, but he was not ready to admit it. John came to check on him fifteen minutes later, but David refused to speak to his leader. John returned to the game, leaving David to his self-imposed ostracism.

Another quarter of an hour passed. The game continued as David sat. John came back again to check on the exile. He dropped to the grass beside him. "Feeling any different?" he asked gently.

David nodded and blinked. "I'm sorry," he said in a subdued voice. "I don't know what is wrong with me. I don't want to get mad. I try not to do it. But then something happens, and I get mad without thinking."

"I know what's wrong," John told him softly.

David looked at him skeptically. "You do?"

"Yes, David. You're just like all the rest of us. You have a sin nature. You will never overcome your temper as long as you are trying to do it by yourself. You need to ask Jesus to come into your heart. He can help you get rid of your temper and the trouble it makes for you."

"How do you know?"

"He did it for me."

"You were never as bad as me."

"I was worse, because I had parents that taught me what was right and wrong. I deliberately went against what I knew the Bible said. My sins piled up on me until I was so miserable I couldn't see any way out. I made such a mess of my life I didn't know if God would even want me. But I told Him if He wanted my life He could have it. I couldn't run it by myself, and I was tired of trying. He took all my sins away and made me a new person. He will do that for you, too, if you ask Him to."

David sat, looking at the grass between his legs. He had heard the plan of salvation explained in terms he understood. He knew it was what he needed, but he struggled against the conviction within.

John laid a hand on David's knee. "Would you like to ask Him?"

The love in the touch and the gentle pleading of the voice dissolved the last resistance in David's heart. He nodded, sniffed, and wiped the back of his hand across his eyes.

"Then let's do it now," John suggested.

"Here?"

"Certainly," John assured him. "God will hear just as well out here as in chapel."

The two heads bowed under the open canopy of the heavens. The prayer of the penitent soul was heard and answered instantly. John's prayer followed, asking blessing and strength on this new son of God. Their praying took only a few minutes, but the implications of those moments would last into eternity.

David was not the first boy John had led to Christ, nor would he be the last. But David's conversion was one of the most outstanding because of the total change it made in his life. He was no longer aggressive and violent. Instead, he radiated joy, eagerly participated in all the activities of camp life and shared his faith with anyone who would listen. If John had not seen the change taking place before his eyes he would have found it hard to believe this was the same David who had once tried to appear aloof, scornful, and tough. He had found the Unchangeable One with whom he could build a lasting relationship. He belonged to someone at last, Someone who would never let him down.

Chapter 35

"I called you to my office this morning to discuss the plans we have been making to give programs at several churches," Marlin told John. "I will be going on a promotional tour for about ten days the beginning of next month. I would like you and several boys to accompany me."

"That sounds exciting," John said enthusiastically. "Where will we be going?"

"We will leave here on the second of next month, heading first for South Carolina. From there we will go to Virginia, Maryland, Delaware, Pennsylvania, Ohio, and Indiana. We will give basically the same program at all of these places."

"What did you want the boys and me to do?" John asked.

"I will outline the work and needs of our

school," Marlin explained. "Then I'd like you and the boys to give your testimonies. Perhaps you could share your call to the work here and what is involved in being a group leader. Then the boys could give short testimonies of how our school has helped them. You will, of course, be leader to these boys on the tour, so I will let you choose the ones who will go along."

"How many boys do you want to take?"

"Three or four. No more than four," Marlin said. "Choose those who have found Christ here at New Hope and are able to give a clear testimony of the change the Lord has made in their lives."

"That means David Hinton for certain," John said thoughtfully.

"Take your time and think it over," Marlin said. "Ask the other group leaders which of their boys they would recommend for this. When you have decided, let me know, and we will discuss it with the boys."

Dennis Hunter and Scott Koller were just as excited as David Hinton when they learned they had been chosen to go on the tour. Not only would the trip be exciting for them, but it was an honor to have been chosen out of the thirty boys at New Hope. John looked forward to the trip, too. He was eager to tell of the desperate needs of emo-

363

tionally damaged boys and urge more young men to give themselves to help in the work. They would be going into his home area and the opportunity to see his family as well as many old friends was an added bonus.

It was an excited group who piled into the van and drove out of the entrance of New Hope Wilderness Camp School in the early morning hours. They had a tight schedule and would have to keep moving. The boys were apprehensive and a little shy at the first meeting. Until they arrived at the place where they were to give the first program, they had not thought about what it would mean to speak before a group of strangers. It was a new experience for them. But as the experience was repeated daily, the boys lost some of their initial bashfulness and spoke more freely. It gave John special joy to hear David share his testimony. Dennis and Scott had never been in John's group. Though they were also outstanding examples of the success of the school, John had come to consider David his own son in the faith. There was a closeness between them he had not experienced with the other boys in his group. David had found in John the love and example he had never received from his natural father.

The tight schedule and exertion of travel

produced some strain and fatigue as the trip progressed. Being in his home area was one of the highlights of the trip for John. When his mother had learned they were coming, she had arranged to have her whole family together for a meal. The twins were young ladies now and the only two of the seven Shenk children still living at home. But as the table boards had been removed over the years to accommodate the smaller number who gathered around it, the size of the family had actually grown. Ida was in her element now as the table was stretched to its full length to accommodate all her family members and guests as well. Becky and Ken were there with their five children, the oldest fast approaching adolescence. Marlin and Jane now had three children, ascending in size like stairsteps. Jim and his wife had three children also and Carl's little family would soon increase by one the number of grandchildren around the big table.

John looked around the table at all the happy faces assembled there. His gaze was drawn more than once to Becky's son who was the same age as his own Todd. Chris was not Todd, he knew, but he always took special notice of Chris's growth and actions, imagining Todd was much the same. Where was Todd? How big was he? What was he like? Would he ever find his son again? He had answers to none of these questions now, and he knew he may never have them. That was in God's Hands.

Concern for Todd was the one ache he would carry through life that would never ease with time. Now he clearly saw the deception of the "new morality" that said immorality was all right as long as it did not hurt anyone. Though it had seemed so right at the time, sin had drawn him into its web, producing a son that was the innocent victim of those sins. The one he had hurt did not yet exist when the sin was committed. But Todd had been hurt just the same. Forgiveness of sin was full and complete, but the scars remained.

"More pie, John?" His mother's question returned John to reality.

"No, thanks, Mom. I couldn't eat another bite, even of the best lemon meringue pie made by the best cook in the country," John grinned. He turned to David. "Try this fellow. His stomach is a bottomless pit."

David took the pie and eyed the wedge appreciatively. "I hate to let it go to waste," he joked. "If you're sure you don't want it."

"I'm sure," John laughed as David speared the point with his fork. "If it's going to go to waist, it may as well go to yours."

David's sigh of pleasure was lost in the roar of the half dozen or more simultaneous conversations being carried on around the table. Seeing David enjoying his mother's cooking was as satisfying for John as eating it himself.

The last stop on the tour was at an Amish Mennonite Church in Indiana. It was nearing starting time and the church was fairly well filled when the New Hope van arrived. John and his boys took places on the front benches as usual and listened to the same type of presentation they had heard Marlin give at every other place they had visited. Then the boys went forward together to give their testimonies. Dennis was first, then Scott, and finally David. Briefly, David described the kind of home from which he had come and the way in which he had come to New Hope.

"I have been in a lot of different homes and institutions in my life," David said. "But I never really felt wanted or like I belonged. When I first came to New Hope, I thought it was just another place I had to go. I was determined not to let myself like it. I thought I'd soon move on to another place. John Shenk was my group leader. I gave him a hard time for awhile. But he kept right on loving me and trying to help me no matter

367

how much trouble I made for him. I could see he was a real Christian, and I wanted to be like him. I tried for awhile to do it myself, but I couldn't. Then John showed me I could never be good enough to be a Christian. I had to let Jesus come and live in my heart. He could do for me what I couldn't do for myself. John has been like a real father to me. I can never thank him and New Hope Wilderness Camp School enough for showing me the way to Christ and making my life worth living."

John rose to share some of his experiences at New Hope and extend a plea for more workers to help in the great need. "It costs the state many times more to keep a man in jail for one year than what it costs us at New Hope to help a boy for the same amount of time. We provide more than shelter and food. We give the boys the Gospel and help them find life in Christ. The majority of our boys leave New Hope and return to society as law abiding citizens and quite often as Christians who become active members of their local churches. If we can rescue these boys before they become hardened criminals, we are saving the state thousands of dollars it would cost to keep them in the penitentiary. More important than the money we are saving the state is to spare these boys from the grief and heartache a life of sin would have brought them. The sooner we can snatch them from the grasp of Satan, the more trouble they are spared.

"From my own experience I can assure you sin exacts a dreadful price. I have done some things I can never undo and I will always regret. I know God has forgiven my sins, but the scars are still with me. I had the advantage of a Christian home. I knew the Word of God and the way back to the Lord. These boys do not have that advantage and will not find the way unless someone tells them."

"There is so much to be done. There is so little time to do it before the Lord returns, and so few are willing to do it. Come to New Hope and help us. You young men, consider spending a year or two in some type of service as a viable option before you start your own homes. Going into service will be more difficult after you have wives and families. Most times it never happens. Our program offers a wonderful opportunity to serve the Lord and the church while you help boys who desperately need help. I can assure you, you will receive a great blessing in your own life, and you will never regret the time you spend in service."

At the conclusion of the service, John and

Marlin stood behind a table of literature and information on New Hope Wilderness Camp School, to meet the people of the congregation and to answer any questions they might have. John had met so many people in the last week he knew it was hopeless to try to remember them all. The line moved slowly past the table as people stopped to visit and share their appreciation for the work the school was doing.

John saw him coming before he reached the table. The bearded face looked familiar, but John had no name to match with it. Ahead of the man walked a slightly plump woman wearing a modest, plain-colored dress and a square white covering on her head. She carried a baby boy in her arms. Beside her was a girl about six years of age and another boy of about four was sandwiched between the couple.

The man stopped at the end of the table. "John!" he said simply, in a voice choked with emotion.

Not until he spoke did John know who he was. "Sam!" Emotion sealed their lips momentarily. Then a torrent of words tangled as the long-lost friends both spoke at once. "How did you—" "This is a—" They laughed and stopped speaking.

"I never expected to see you here," John

began again.

"And I had no idea you would be here either when I came tonight," Sam said. "I lost track of you, but I never stopped praying for you. I could hardly believe my eyes when I saw you walk in with the boys. The last I heard you had married Lynette."

John's eyes clouded. "Yes, we were married for over three years," he admitted. "She divorced me and took away our son. It was a painful way to learn, but through it all the Lord brought me back to Himself."

Sam's eyes overflowed with tears. "You can't imagine how I feel to know my prayers for you are answered. All these years I've lived with the regrets and scars of my sins. The knowledge that I led you astray has tormented me day and night. I couldn't forgive myself for what I did to you. But the Lord is still faithful and merciful."

"Amen!" John agreed. "Only God can turn sorrow into joy and give beauty for ashes. It's a miracle of grace. And now tell me how you came to be here. I knew you were from Indiana, but do you live near here?"

"This is our home church," Sam explained, introducing John to the woman beside him. "My wife, Dolores, was from this church, and I joined here with her before we were married."

"It's nice meeting you," John acknowledged the introduction. "And I presume this is your family?"

"Yes," Dolores answered, giving each of the children's names as she pointed them out with her eyes.

"You have a nice family. I'm so glad I met you here," John responded cordially.

"I wish we had more time to talk," Sam lamented. "If I had known you were with this group, I would have insisted on putting you up for the night."

"That would have been nice," John agreed wistfully. "I wish, too, we had more time. We have a lot of catching up to do. But we are planning to head straight from here to Alabama. We'll be driving most of the night to keep our schedule."

"If you ever get back to Indiana again, let me know ahead of time, and we'll arrange to have you in our home," Sam promised.

"I'll do that," John assured him as the line moved on, carrying Sam and his family with it. "You're always welcome to visit us in Alabama, too," he called after Sam.

"I'd love to do that," Sam called back with a wave of his hand.

As the crowd dwindled and people left for their homes, John and the boys began packing their material for the last time. The trip had been exciting, but it would be good to get back home again. Home? Yes, New Hope was home. Home because his heart was there. Through winding ways, God had brought him to completeness in the center of His will.

I never stopped praying for you. Sam's words echoed in John's head. How many petitions had gone to the throne on his behalf, he had no idea. Gratitude for all those who had cared enough to continue to pray for years welled up in his heart and overflowed in his own silent prayer of thanksgiving and praise to the God of his salvation. Though he had stepped out of God's will, he had never been out of the circle of His love.

John closed the lid on the last box of literature, picked it up, and started for the door. "That's it, boys," he said. "Let's head for home."

Christian Light Publications, Inc., is a nonprofit, conservative Mennonite publishing company providing Christ-centered, Biblical literature including books, Gospel tracts, Sunday school materials, summer Bible school materials, and a full curriculum for Christian day schools and homeschools. Though produced primarily in English, some books, tracts, and school materials are also available in Spanish.

For more information about the ministry of CLP or its publications, or for spiritual help, please contact us at:

Christian Light Publications, Inc.
P. O. Box 1212
Harrisonburg, VA 22803-1212

Telephone—540-434-0768
Fax—540-433-8896
E-mail—info@clp.org
www.clp.org